Advanced Equity Derivatives

Founded in 1807, John Wiley & Sons is the oldest independent publishing company in the United States. With offices in North America, Europe, Australia and Asia, Wiley is globally committed to developing and marketing print and electronic products and services for our customers' professional and personal knowledge and understanding.

The Wiley Finance series contains books written specifically for finance and investment professionals as well as sophisticated individual investors and their financial advisors. Book topics range from portfolio management to e-commerce, risk management, financial engineering, valuation and financial instrument analysis, as well as much more.

For a list of available titles, visit our website at www.WileyFinance.com.

Advanced Equity Derivatives

Volatility and Correlation

SÉBASTIEN BOSSU

WILEY

Library of Congress Cataloging-in-Publication Data:

Bossu, Sébastien.
  Advanced equity derivatives : volatility and correlation / Sébastien Bossu.
    pages cm. – (Wiley finance series)
  Includes bibliographical references and index.
  ISBN 978-1-118-75096-4 (cloth); ISBN 978-1-118-77484-7 (ePDF);
ISBN 978-1-118-77471-7 (ePub)
  1. Derivative securities. I. Title.
  HG6024.A3B67 2014
  332.64'57–dc23
                                              2013046823

Printed in the United States of America.

10 9 8 7 6 5 4 3 2 1

*"As for the expense," gravely declared
the deputy Haffner who never opened his mouth
except on great occasions, "our children will pay for it,
and nothing will be more just."*

Emile Zola, *La Curée* (*The Kill*)

Contents

Foreword

I am pleased to introduce Sébastien Bossu's new book, *Advanced Equity Derivatives*, which is a great contribution to the literature in our field. Years of practical experience as an exotics structurer, combined with strong theoretical skills, allowed Sébastien to write a condensed yet profound text on a variety of advanced topics: volatility derivatives and volatility trading, correlation modeling, dispersion trading, local and stochastic volatility models, to name just a few.

This book not only reviews the most important concepts and recent developments in option pricing and modeling, but also offers insightful explications of great relevance to researchers as well as traders. For instance, readers will find formulas to overhedge convex payoffs, the derivation of Feller conditions for the Heston model, or an exposition of the latest local correlation models to correctly price basket options.

Perhaps the most exciting aspect of this book is its treatment of the latest generation of equity derivatives, namely volatility and correlation derivatives. Readers will find a wealth of information on these new securities, including original analyses and models to approach their valuation. The chapters on correlation are particularly commendable, as they shed light on an otherwise still obscure area.

The content quality, selection of topics, and level of insight truly set this book apart. I have no doubt that equity derivatives practitioners around the world, be they traders, quants or investors, will find it extremely pertinent, and I wish this book every success.

Peter Carr

Dr. Peter Carr has over 18 years of experience in the derivatives industry and is currently Global Head of Market Modeling at Morgan Stanley, as well as Executive Director of the Math Finance program at NYU's Courant Institute. He has over 70 publications in academic and industry-oriented journals and serves as an associate editor for eight journals related to mathematical finance. Dr. Carr is also the Treasurer of the Bachelier Finance Society, a trustee for the Museum of Mathematics in New York, and has received numerous awards, including Quant of the Year by Risk *magazine in 2003, the ISA Medal for Science in 2008, and Financial Engineer of the Year in 2010.*

Preface

In 2004, while working as an equity derivatives analyst at J.P. Morgan in London, I came upon an esoteric trade: someone was simultaneously selling correlation and buying it back for a (risky) profit using two different methods. I became obsessed with the rationale behind this trade, and, after writing down the math, I discovered with excitement that with some corrections this trade led to a pure dynamic arbitrage strategy—the kind you normally find only in textbooks.

I could see, however, that transaction costs and other market frictions made the strategy very hard to implement in practice, especially for price takers on the buy side. But the fact remained that correlation could be bought and sold at very different prices, and that didn't make sense to me. So I developed a simple "toy" model to see how this gap might be accounted for, and as I suspected I found that there should be little difference. What this meant is that one of the two correlation instruments involved in the trade, namely the correlation swap, was not priced at "fair value" according to my analysis.

Later on I refined my model, which I introduce in the last chapter of this book among other topics, and reached similar conclusions. I am very pleased that the topic of equity correlation has gained tremendous momentum since 2004, and it is one of this book's ambitions to introduce the work of others in this highly specialized field. I have no doubt that many new exciting results are yet to be discovered in the coming years.

I also wanted to cover other key advanced concepts in equity derivatives that are relevant to traders, quantitative analysts, and other professionals. Many of these concepts, such as implied distributions and local volatilities, are now well-known and established in the field, while others, such as local and stochastic correlation, lie at the forefront of current research.

To get the most out of this book, readers must already be familiar with the terminology and standard pricing theory of equity derivatives, which can be found in my textbook *Introduction to Equity Derivatives: Theory & Practice*, second edition, also published by John Wiley & Sons.

I relied on a fair amount of advanced mathematics, and therefore a graduate scientific education is a prerequisite here, especially for those readers who want to solve the problems included at the end of each chapter.

The book is made of nine chapters, which are meant to be read sequentially, starting with an exposition of the most widespread exotic derivatives and culminating with cutting-edge concepts on stochastic correlation, which are necessary to correctly price the next generation of equity derivatives such as correlation swaps.

Some simplifications, such as zero interest rates and dividends, were often necessary to avoid convoluted mathematical expressions. I strongly encourage readers to check the particular assumptions used for each formula before transposing it into another context.

I hope this book will prove insightful and useful to its target audience. I am always interested to hear feedback; please do not hesitate to contact me to share your thoughts.

Acknowledgments

I would like to thank Peter Carr for his foreword, and David Hait and his team at OptionMetrics for providing me with very useful option data. I am grateful to my team at Wiley—Bill Falloon, Meg Freeborn, and associates—for their guidance and professionalism throughout the publication process.

Many thanks also to a group of individuals who, directly or indirectly, made this book possible: Romain Barc, Martin Bertsch, Eynour Boutia, Jose Casino, Mauro Cesa, John Dattorro, Emanuel Derman, Jim Gatheral, Fabrice Rouah, Simone Russo, Roberto Silvotti, and Paul Wilmott.

Last, a special mention to John Lyttle at Ogee Group for his help on many figures and problem solutions.

Advanced Equity
Derivatives

CHAPTER 1

Exotic Derivatives

Strictly speaking, an exotic derivative is any derivative that is not a plain vanilla call or put. In this chapter we review the payoff and properties of the most widespread equity derivative exotics.

1-1   SINGLE-ASSET EXOTICS

1-1.1   Digital Options

A **European digital** or **binary option** pays off $1 if the underlying asset price is above the strike K at maturity T, and 0 otherwise:

$$\text{Digital Payoff} = \begin{cases} 1 & \text{if } S_T > K \\ 0 & \text{otherwise} \end{cases}$$

In its American version, which is more uncommon, the option pays off $1 *as soon as* the strike level is hit.

The Black-Scholes price formula for a digital option is simply:

$$e^{-rT}N(d_2) = e^{-rT}N\left(\frac{\ln(F/K) - \frac{1}{2}\sigma^2 T}{\sigma\sqrt{T}}\right)$$

where F is the forward price of S for maturity T, r is the continuous interest rate, and σ is the volatility parameter. When there is an implied volatility smile this formula is inaccurate and a corrective term must be added (see Section 2-1.3).

Digital options are not easy to dynamically hedge because their delta can become very large near maturity. Exotic traders tend to overhedge them with a tight call spread whose range may be determined according to several possible empirical rules, such as:

- *Daily volatility rule*: Set the range to match a typical stock price move over one day. For example, if the annual volatility of the underlying stock is 32% annually; that is, $32\%/\sqrt{252} \approx 2\%$ daily, a digital option struck at $100 would be overhedged with $98–$100 call spreads.
- *Normalized liquidity rule*: Set the range so that the quantity of call spreads is in line with the market liquidity of call spreads with 5% range. The quantity of call spreads is N/R where N is the quantity of digitals and R is the call spread range. If the tradable quantity of call spreads with range 5% is V, the normalized tradable quantity of call spreads with range R would be $V \times R / 0.05$. Solving for R gives $R = \sqrt{0.05 \times \frac{N}{V}}$. In practice V is either provided by the option trader or estimated using the daily trading volume of the stock.

1-1.2 Asian Options

In an **Asian call** or **put**, the final underlying asset price is replaced by an average:

$$\text{Asian Call Payoff} = \max(0, A_T - K)$$
$$\text{Asian Put Payoff} = \max(0, K - A_T)$$

where $A_T = \frac{1}{n} \sum_{i=1}^{n} S_{t_i}$ for a set of pre-agreed fixing dates $t_1 < t_2 < \cdots < t_n \leq T$. For example, a one-year at-the-money Asian call on the S&P 500 index with quarterly fixings pays off $\max\left(0, \frac{S_{0.25}+S_{0.5}+S_{0.75}+S_1}{4} - S_0\right)$, where S_0 is the current spot price and $S_{0.25}, \ldots, S_1$ are the future spot prices observed every three months.

On occasion, the strike may also be replaced by an average, typically over a short initial observation period.

Fixed-strike Asian options are always cheaper than their European counterparts, because A_T is less volatile than S_T.

There is no closed-form Black-Scholes formula for arithmetic Asian options. However, for geometric Asian options where $A_T = \exp\left[\frac{1}{T}\int_0^T \ln S_t \, dt\right]$, the Black-Scholes formulas may be used with adjusted volatility $\hat{\sigma} = \sigma/\sqrt{3}$ and dividend yield $\hat{q} = \frac{1}{2}\left(r + q + \frac{\sigma^2}{6}\right)$, as shown in Problem 1.3.

A common numerical approximation for the price of arithmetic Asian options is obtained by fitting a lognormal distribution to the actual risk-neutral moments of A_T.

1-1.3 Barrier Options

In a **barrier call** or **put**, the underlying asset price must hit, or never hit, a certain barrier level H before maturity:

- For a knock-in option, the underlying must hit the barrier, or else the option pays nothing.
- For a knock-out option, the underlying must *never* hit the barrier, or else the option pays nothing.

Barrier options are always cheaper than their European counterparts, because their payoff is subject to an additional constraint. On occasion, a fixed cash "rebate" is paid out if the barrier condition is not met.

Similar to digital options, barrier options are not easy to dynamically hedge: their delta can become very large near the barrier level. Exotic traders tend to overhedge them by shifting the barrier a little in their valuation model.

Continuously monitored barrier options have closed-form Black-Scholes formulas, which can be found, for instance, in Hull (2012). The preferred pricing approach is the local volatility model (see Chapter 4).

In practice the barrier is often monitored on a set of pre-agreed fixing dates $t_1 < t_2 < \cdots < t_n \leq T$. Monte Carlo simulations are then commonly used for valuation.

Broadie, Glasserman, and Kou (1997) derived a nice result to switch between continuous and discrete barrier monitoring by shifting the barrier level H by a factor $\exp(\pm\beta\sigma\sqrt{\Delta t})$ where $\beta \approx 0.5826$, σ is the underlying volatility, and Δt is the time between two fixing dates.

1-1.4 Lookback Options

A **lookback call** or **put** is an option on the maximum or minimum price reached by the underlying asset until maturity:

$$\text{Lookback call payoff} = \max(0, \max_{0 \leq t \leq T} S_t - K);$$

$$\text{Lookback put payoff} = \max(0, K - \min_{0 \leq t \leq T} S_t).$$

Lookback options are always more expensive than their European counterparts: about twice as much when the strike is nearly at the money, as shown in Problem 1.5.

Continuously monitored lookback options have closed-form Black-Scholes formulas, which can be found, for instance, in Hull (2012). The preferred pricing approach is the local volatility model (see Chapter 4).

In practice the maximum or minimum is often monitored on a set of pre-agreed fixing dates $t_1 < t_2 < \cdots < t_n \leq T$. Monte Carlo simulations are then commonly used for valuation.

1-1.5   Forward Start Options

In a **forward start option** the strike is determined as a percentage k of the spot price on a future start date $t_0 > 0$:

$$\text{Forward start call payoff} = \max(0, S_T - kS_{t_0});$$

$$\text{Forward start put payoff} = \max(0, kS_{t_0} - S_T).$$

At $t = t_0$ a forward start option becomes a regular option. Note that the forward start feature is not specific to vanilla options and can be added to any exotic option that has a strike.

Forward start options have closed-form Black-Scholes formulas. The preferred pricing approach is to use a stochastic volatility model (see Chapter 4).

1-1.6   Cliquet Options

A **cliquet** or **ratchet option** consists of a series of consecutive forward start options, for example:

$$\text{Monthly cliquet option payoff} = \max\left[0, \sum_{i=1}^{12} \min\left(5\%, \frac{S_{i/12}}{S_{(i-1)/12}} - 1\right)\right]$$

where 5% is the local cap amount. In other words, this particular cliquet option pays off the greater of zero and the sum of monthly returns, each capped at 5%.

Cliquet options can be very difficult to value and especially hedge.

1-2   MULTI-ASSET EXOTICS

Multi-asset exotics are based on several underlying stocks or indices, and thus their fair value depends on the level of correlation between the underlying assets. They are typically priced on a Monte Carlo simulation engine with local volatilities (see Chapter 4 and Chapter 6, Section 6-5).

1-2.1   Spread Options

The payoff of a **spread option** is based on the difference in gross return between two underlying assets:

$$\text{Spread option payoff} = \max\left(0, \frac{S_T^{(1)}}{S_0^{(1)}} - \frac{S_T^{(2)}}{S_0^{(2)}} - k\right)$$

where k is the residual strike level (in %). For example, a spread option on Apple Inc. vs Google Inc. with 5% strike pays off the outperformance of Apple over Google in excess of 5%: if Apple's return is 13% and Google's is 4%, the option pays off $13\% - 4\% - 5\% = 4\%$.

The value of a spread option is very sensitive to the level of correlation between the two assets. Specifically the option value increases as correlation decreases: the lower the correlation, the wider the two assets are expected to spread apart.

In practice hedging spread options can be difficult because the spread $\frac{S_T^{(1)}}{S_0^{(1)}} - \frac{S_T^{(2)}}{S_0^{(2)}}$ is often nearly orthogonal to the basket $\frac{1}{2}\left[\frac{S_T^{(1)}}{S_0^{(1)}} + \frac{S_T^{(2)}}{S_0^{(2)}}\right] - 1$.

When $k = 0$ a spread option is also known as an exchange option. A closed-form Black-Scholes formula is then available which can be found, for instance, in Hull (2012).

1-2.2 Basket Options

A **basket call** or **put** is an option on the gross return of a portfolio of n underlying assets:

$$\text{Basket call payoff} = \max\left(0, \sum_{i=1}^{n} w_i \frac{S_T^{(i)}}{S_0^{(i)}} - k\right);$$

$$\text{Basket put payoff} = \max\left(0, k - \sum_{i=1}^{n} w_i \frac{S_T^{(i)}}{S_0^{(i)}}\right),$$

where the weights $w_1, \ldots, w_n$ sum to 100% and the strike k is expressed as a percentage (e.g., 100% for at the money).

EXAMPLE

Equally-Weighted Stock Basket Call

Option seller: ABC Bank Co.
Notional amount: $20,000,000
Issue date: [Today]
Maturity date: [Today + 3 years]

(Continued)

EXAMPLE (*Continued*)

Equally-Weighted Stock Basket Call

Underlying stocks: IBM (IBM), Microsoft (MSFT), Google (GOOG)
Payoff:

$$\text{Notional} \times \max\left(0, \frac{1}{3}\left(\frac{IBM_{\text{final}}}{IBM_{\text{initial}}} + \frac{MSFT_{\text{final}}}{MSFT_{\text{initial}}} + \frac{GOOG_{\text{final}}}{GOOG_{\text{initial}}}\right) - 1\right)$$

Option price: 17.4%

The value of a basket option is sensitive to the level of pairwise correlations between the assets. The lower the correlation, the less volatile the portfolio and the cheaper the basket option.

Basket options do not have closed-form Black-Scholes formulas. A common approximation technique is to fit a lognormal distribution to the actual moments of the basket and then use formulas for the single-asset case.

1-2.3   Worst-Of and Best-Of Options

A **worst-of call** or **put** is an option on the lowest gross return between n underlying assets:

$$\text{Worst-of call payoff} = \max\left(0, \min_{1 \le i \le n} \frac{S_T^{(i)}}{S_0^{(i)}} - k\right);$$

$$\text{Worst-of put payoff} = \max\left(0, k - \min_{1 \le i \le n} \frac{S_T^{(i)}}{S_0^{(i)}}\right),$$

where the strike k is expressed as a percentage (e.g., 100% for at the money). For example, a worst-of at-the-money call on Apple, Google, and Microsoft pays off the worst stock return between the three companies, if positive.

Similarly, a **best-of call** or **put** is an option on the highest gross return between n underlying assets.

Worst-of calls and best-of puts are always cheaper than any of their single-asset European counterparts, while best-of calls and worst-of puts are always more expensive.

1-2.4   Quanto Options

The payoff of a **quanto option** is paid out in a different currency from the underlying assets, at a guaranteed exchange rate. For example, a call on the S&P 500 index quanto euro pays off $\max(0, S_T - K)$ in euros instead of dollars, thereby guaranteeing an exchange rate of 1 euro per dollar.

The actual exchange rate between the asset currency and the quanto currency is in fact an implicit additional underlying asset. The value of quanto options is very sensitive to the correlation between the primary asset and the implicit exchange rate.

Quanto options are an example of hybrid exotic options involving different asset classes—here equity and foreign exchange.

In terms of pricing, the quanto feature is often approached using a technique called change of numeraire. In summary, this technique says that the risk-neutral dynamics of an asset quantoed in a different currency from its natural currency has the same volatility coefficient but an adjusted drift coefficient.

FOCUS ON CHANGE OF NUMERAIRE

This technique builds upon the concepts of change of measure and Girsanov's theorem, which are explained in Appendix 1.A.

Consider a world with two currencies, say dollars and euros, and a non-income-paying asset S with dollar price $S^{\$}$ and euro price $S^{€}$. Denote X the exchange rate of one dollar into euros, so that $S^{€}_t = S^{\$}_t X_t$. Assume that $S^{\$}$ and X both follow a geometric Brownian motion under the dollar risk-neutral measure $\mathbb{Q}^{\$}$, specifically:

$$\text{For } S^{\$}: \; dS^{\$}_t / S^{\$}_t = r_{\$} dt + \sigma dW_t$$

$$\text{For } X: \; dX_t / X_t = v dt + \eta dZ_t$$

where W, Z are standard Brownian motions under $\mathbb{Q}^{\$}$ with correlation ρ, $r_{\$}$ is the dollar interest rate, and all other parameters are free.

Because the original Girsanov theorem applies to independent Brownian motions, we rewrite $Z = \rho W + \bar{\rho} W^{\perp}$ where $W^{\perp}$ is a standard Brownian motion under $\mathbb{Q}^{\$}$ independent from W and $\bar{\rho} = \sqrt{1 - \rho^2}$ is the orthogonal complement of ρ. The diffusion equation for X then becomes:

$$dX_t / X_t = v dt + \eta \rho dW_t + \eta \bar{\rho} dW_t^{\perp}$$

Applying the Ito-Doeblin theorem to the product $S_t^{\euro} = S_t^{\$} X_t$ we obtain after simplifying:

$$dS_t^{\euro}/S_t^{\euro} = (r_{\$} + v + \rho\sigma\eta)dt + (\sigma + \rho\eta)dW_t + \eta\bar{\rho}dW_t^{\perp} \qquad (1.1)$$

Because $S^{\euro}$ is a euro tradable asset we must also have:

$$dS_t^{\euro}/S_t^{\euro} = r_{\euro}dt + (\sigma + \rho\eta)d\tilde{W}_t + \eta\bar{\rho}d\tilde{W}_t^{\perp} \qquad (1.2)$$

where $\tilde{W}, \tilde{W}^{\perp}$ are independent standard Brownian motions under the euro risk-neutral measure $\mathbb{Q}^{\euro}$. This is the diffusion equation of the *composite* asset $S^{\euro}$ after conversion from dollars to euros.

The processes $\tilde{W}, \tilde{W}^{\perp}$ are affine transformations of the original processes $W, W^{\perp}$; specifically:

$$\begin{cases} \tilde{W}_t = W_t + \gamma_1 t \\ \tilde{W}_t^{\perp} = W_t^{\perp} + \gamma_2 t \end{cases}$$

where γ_1 and γ_2 are particular coefficients. Substituting into Equation (1.1) and connecting with Equation (1.2) we obtain that γ_1, γ_2 must satisfy:

$$r_{\$} + v + \rho\sigma\eta = r_{\euro} + \gamma_1(\sigma + \rho\eta) + \gamma_2\eta\bar{\rho}$$

In order to determine γ_1, γ_2 uniquely, we need another equation. This is provided by the dynamics of X, which is a euro-tradable asset (it is the price in euros of \$1):

$$dX_t/X_t = (r_{\euro} - r_{\$})dt + \eta\rho d\tilde{W}_t + \eta\bar{\rho}d\tilde{W}_t^{\perp}$$

Following the same reasoning we find that γ_1, γ_2 must also satisfy:

$$v = r_{\euro} - r_{\$} + \gamma_1\eta\rho + \gamma_2\eta\bar{\rho}$$

Solving for γ_1, γ_2 we find:

$$\begin{cases} \gamma_1 = \eta\rho \\ \gamma_2 = \dfrac{v + r_{\$} - r_{\euro} - \eta^2\rho^2}{\eta\bar{\rho}} \end{cases}$$

The dynamics of $S^{\$}$ may thus be rewritten as:

$$dS_t^{\$}/S_t^{\$} = r_{\$}dt + \sigma dW_t = r_{\$}dt + \sigma(d\tilde{W}_t - \gamma_1 dt) = (r_{\$} - \rho\sigma\eta)dt + \sigma d\tilde{W}_t$$

This is the diffusion equation for $S^{\$}$ quanto euro. In particular, the forward price of $S^{\$}$ quanto euro is:

$$\mathbb{E}^{\mathbb{Q}^{\epsilon}}(S_T^{\$}) = S_0^{\$} e^{(r_{\$} - \rho \sigma \eta)T}$$

1-3 STRUCTURED PRODUCTS

Structured products combine several securities together, especially exotic options. They are typically sold as equity-linked notes (ELN) or mutual funds to small investors as well as large institutions. These notes and funds are sometimes traded on exchanges.

EXAMPLES

Capital Guaranteed Performance Note

Issuer: ABC Bank Co.
Notional amount: $10,000,000
Issue date: [Today]
Maturity date: [Today + 5 years]
Underlying index: S&P 500 (SPX)

Payoff:

$$\text{Notional} \times \left[100\% + \text{Participation} \times \max\left(0, \frac{SPX_{\text{final}}}{SPX_{\text{initial}}} - 1 \right) \right]$$

Participation: 50%

Reverse Convertible Note

Issuer: ABC Bank Co.
Notional amount: €2,000,000
Issue date: [Today]
Maturity date: [Today + 3 years]
Underlying stock: Kroger Co. (KR)

Payoff:

(a) If, between the start and maturity dates, Kroger Co. always trades above the Barrier level, Issuer will pay:

$$\text{Notional} \times \max\left(115\%, \frac{S_{\text{final}}}{S_{\text{initial}}} \right)$$

(b) Otherwise, Issuer will pay:

$$\text{Notional} \times \frac{S_{\text{final}}}{S_{\text{initial}}}$$

Barrier level: 70%

In the Capital Guaranteed Performance Note, investors are guaranteed[1] to get their \$10 mn capital back after five years. This is much safer than a direct \$10 mn investment in the S&P 500 index, which could result in a loss. In exchange for this protection, investors receive a smaller share in the S&P 500 performance: 50% instead of 100%.

In the Reverse Convertible Note, investors may lose on their €2 mn capital if Kroger Co. ever trades below the 70% barrier, but never more than a direct investment in the stock (ignoring dividends). Otherwise, investors receive at least €2.3 mn after three years, and never less than a direct investment in the stock (again, ignoring dividends).

In some cases it is possible to break down a structured product into a portfolio of securities whose prices are known and find its value. In all other cases the payoff is typically programmed on a Monte Carlo simulation engine.

Multi-asset structured products significantly expand the payoff possibilities of exotic options. They allow investors to play on correlation and express complex investment views.

EXAMPLE

Worst-Of Reverse Convertible Note Quanto CHF

Issuer: ABC Bank Co.
Notional amount: CHF 5,000,000
Issue date: [Today]
Maturity date: [Today + 3 years]
Underlying indexes: S&P 500 (SPX), EuroStoxx-50 (SX5E), Nikkei 225 (NKY)
Payoff:

(a) If, between the start and maturity dates, all underlying indexes always trade above the Barrier level, Issuer will pay:

$$\text{Notional} \times \max\left(120\%, \min\left(\frac{SPX_{\text{final}}}{SPX_{\text{initial}}}, \frac{SX5E_{\text{final}}}{SX5E_{\text{initial}}}, \frac{NKY_{\text{final}}}{NKY_{\text{initial}}}\right)\right)$$

(Continued)

---

[1]Provided the issuer does not go bankrupt.

> **EXAMPLE** (*Continued*)
>
> Worst-Of Reverse Convertible Note Quanto CHF
>
> **(b)** Otherwise, Issuer will pay:
>
> $$\text{Notional} \times \min \left(\frac{SPX_{\text{final}}}{SPX_{\text{initial}}}, \frac{SX5E_{\text{final}}}{SX5E_{\text{initial}}}, \frac{NKY_{\text{final}}}{NKY_{\text{initial}}} \right)$$
>
> Barrier level: 50% of Initial Price

Multi-asset structured product valuation is almost always done using Monte Carlo simulations. Hedging correlation risk is often difficult or expensive, and exotic trading desks tend to accumulate large exposures, which can cause significant losses during a market crash.

REFERENCES

Baxter, Martin, and Andrew Rennie. 1996. *Financial Calculus: An Introduction to Derivative Pricing*. New York: Cambridge University Press.

Broadie, Mark, Paul Glasserman, and Steven Kou. 1997. "A Continuity Correction for Discrete Barrier Options." *Mathematical Finance* 7 (4): 325–348.

Hull, John C. 2012. *Option, Futures, and Other Derivatives*, 8th ed. New York: Prentice Hall.

PROBLEMS

1.1 "Free" Option

Consider a European call option on an underlying asset S with strike K and maturity T where "you only pay the premium if you win," that is, if $S_T > K$.

(a) Draw the diagram of the net P&L of this "free" option at maturity. Is it really "free"?

(b) Find a replicating portfolio for the "free" option using vanilla and exotic options.

(c) Calculate the fair value of the "free" option premium using the Black-Scholes model with 20% volatility, $S_0 = K = \$100$, one-year maturity, zero interest and dividend rates.

1.2 Autocallable

Consider an exotic option expiring in one, two, or three years on an underlying asset S with the following payoff mechanism:

- If after one year $S_1 > S_0$ the option pays off $1 + C$ and terminates;
- Else if after two years $S_2 > S_0$ the option pays off $1 + 2C$ and terminates;
- Else if after three years $S_3 > 0.7 \times S_0$ the option pays off $\max(1 + 3C, S_3/S_0)$;
- Otherwise, the option pays off S_3/S_0.

Assuming $S_0 = \$100$, zero interest and dividend rates, and 25% volatility, estimate the level of C so that the option is worth 1 using Monte Carlo simulations.

1.3 Geometric Asian Option

Consider a geometric Asian option on an underlying S with payoff $f(A_T)$ where $A_T = \exp\left(\frac{1}{T}\int_0^T \ln S_t \, dt\right)$. Assume that S follows a geometric Brownian motion with parameters $(r - q, \sigma)$ under the risk-neutral measure.

(a) Using the Ito-Doeblin theorem, show that

$$A_T = S_0 \exp\left(\frac{1}{2}\left(r - q - \frac{1}{2}\sigma^2\right)T + \frac{\sigma}{T}\int_0^T W_t \, dt\right)$$

(b) Using the Ito-Doeblin theorem, show that $\int_0^T W_t \, dt = \int_0^T (T - t) dW_t$. What is the distribution of this quantity?

(c) Show that A_T is lognormally distributed with parameters $\left(\ln S_0 + \left(r - \hat{q} - \frac{1}{2}\hat{\sigma}^2\right)T, \hat{\sigma}\sqrt{T}\right)$ where $\hat{\sigma} = \sigma/\sqrt{3}$ and $\hat{q} = \frac{1}{2}\left(r + q + \frac{\sigma^2}{6}\right)$.

1.4 Change of Measure

In the context of Appendix 1.A, verify that $\mathbb{E}^{\mathbb{Q}}(S_T) = S_0 e^{rT}$ using the expression for $d\mathbb{Q}/d\mathbb{P}$.

1.5 At-the-Money Lookback Options

The Black-Scholes closed-form formula for an at-the-money lookback call is given as:

$$Lookback_0 = e^{-rT}S_0(N(-\alpha_2) - 1) + S_0 N(\alpha_1)\left(1 + \frac{\sigma^2}{2r}\right) - e^{-rT}\frac{\sigma^2}{2r}S_0 N(\alpha_3)$$

where $\alpha_{1,2} = \left(\frac{r}{\sigma} \pm \frac{1}{2}\sigma\right)\sqrt{T}$ and $\alpha_3 = \left(-\frac{r}{\sigma} + \frac{1}{2}\sigma\right)\sqrt{T}$.

Using a first-order Taylor expansion of the cumulative normal distribution $N(\cdot)$ show that for reasonable rates and maturities we have the proxy:

$$Lookback_0 \approx \frac{4S_0\sigma\sqrt{T}}{\sqrt{2\pi}}$$

which is twice as much as the European call proxy: $c_0 \approx \frac{2S_0\sigma\sqrt{T}}{\sqrt{2\pi}}$.

1.6 Siegel's Paradox

This problem is about foreign exchange rates and goes beyond the scope of equity derivatives.

Consider two currencies, say dollars and euros, and suppose that their corresponding interest rates, $r_\$$ and $r_\euro$, are constant. Let X be the euro–dollar exchange rate defined as the number of dollars per euro. The traditional risk-neutral process for X is thus:

$$dX_t = (r_\$ - r_\euro)X_t dt + \sigma X_t dW_t$$

where W is a standard Brownian motion.

(a) Using the Ito-Doeblin theorem, show that the risk-neutral dynamics for the dollar-euro exchange rate, that is, the number $1/X$ of euros per dollar, is:

$$d\frac{1}{X_t} = (r_\euro - r_\$ + \sigma^2)\frac{1}{X_t}dt + \sigma\frac{1}{X_t}dW_t$$

(b) Symmetry suggests that the drift of $1/X$ should be $r_\euro - r_\$$ instead—this is Siegel's paradox. Use your knowledge of quantos (see Section 1-2.4) to resolve the paradox.

APPENDIX 1.A: CHANGE OF MEASURE AND GIRSANOV'S THEOREM

Recall that the Black-Scholes model assumes that the underlying asset price process follows a geometric Brownian motion:

$$dS_t/S_t = \mu dt + \sigma dW_t$$

where W is a standard Brownian motion under some objective probability measure $\mathbb{P}$, μ is the objective drift coefficient, and σ is the objective volatility coefficient.

However, the drift coefficient μ disappears from option pricing equations as a result of delta-hedging, and option prices may equivalently be calculated as discounted expected payoffs under a special probability measure $\mathbb{Q}$ called risk-neutral. Under $\mathbb{Q}$, the underlying asset price process follows the geometric Brownian motion:

$$dS_t/S_t = rdt + \sigma dW'_t$$

where W' is a standard Brownian motion under $\mathbb{Q}$, r is the continuous interest rate, and σ is the *same* volatility coefficient.

To understand how $\mathbb{P}$ and $\mathbb{Q}$ relate, consider the *un*discounted expected payoff:

$$\mathbb{E}^{\mathbb{Q}}(f(S_T)) = \int_0^\infty f(s)\mathbb{Q}\{S_T = s\}ds$$

$$= \int_0^\infty f(s)\frac{\mathbb{Q}\{S_T = s\}}{\mathbb{P}\{S_T = s\}}\mathbb{P}\{S_T = s\}ds$$

If we define the ratio of densities $h(s) = \frac{\mathbb{Q}\{S_T=s\}}{\mathbb{P}\{S_T=s\}}$ then we can write:

$$\mathbb{E}^{\mathbb{Q}}(f(S_T)) = \int_0^\infty f(s)h(s)\mathbb{P}\{S_T = s\}ds = \mathbb{E}^{\mathbb{P}}(f(S_T)h(S_T)).$$

The change of measure from $\mathbb{P}$ to $\mathbb{Q}$ is thus equivalent to multiplying by the random variable $h(S_T)$ called a Radon-Nikodym derivative and properly denoted $\frac{d\mathbb{Q}}{d\mathbb{P}}$. Girsanov's theorem states that $\mathbb{Q}$ exists and is properly defined by a Radon-Nikodym derivative of the form:

$$\frac{d\mathbb{Q}}{d\mathbb{P}} = \exp\left(\frac{r-\mu}{\sigma}W_T - \frac{1}{2}\left(\frac{r-\mu}{\sigma}\right)^2 T\right)$$

Furthermore, $W'_t = W_t + \frac{r-\mu}{\sigma}t$ is then a Brownian motion under $\mathbb{Q}$. Problem 1.4 verifies that $\mathbb{E}^{\mathbb{Q}}(S_T) = S_0 e^{rT}$.

For a rigorous yet accessible exposition of the change of measure technique and Girsanov's theorem we refer the reader to Baxter and Rennie (1996).

CHAPTER 2

The Implied Volatility Surface

Despite its flaws and limitations, the Black-Scholes model became the benchmark to interpret option prices. Specifically, option prices are reverse-engineered to calculate implied volatilities, the same way that bond prices are transformed into yields, which are easier to understand. This process, combined with interpolation and extrapolation techniques, gives rise to an entire surface along the strike and maturity dimensions.

2-1 THE IMPLIED VOLATILITY SMILE AND ITS CONSEQUENCES

The Black-Scholes model assumes a single constant volatility parameter to price options. In practice, however, every listed vanilla option has a different implied volatility $\sigma^*(K, T)$ for each strike K and maturity T. Figure 2.1 shows what an implied volatility surface $(K, T) \mapsto \sigma^*(K, T)$ looks like.

For a fixed maturity T the curve $K \mapsto \sigma^*(K, T)$ is called the implied volatility smile or skew and exhibits a downward-sloping shape, as shown in Figure 2.2. Note that in other asset classes, such as interest rates or currencies, the smile tends to be symmetric rather than downward-sloping.

2-1.1 Consequence for the Pricing of Call and Put Spreads

A direct consequence of the implied volatility smile is that the Black-Scholes model gives inaccurate call spread and put spread prices. To illustrate this point, Figure 2.3 shows the Black-Scholes price of a one-year call spread with strikes $100 and $110 as a function of the single Black-Scholes volatility

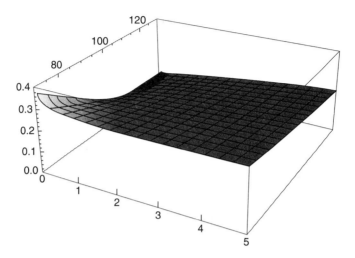

FIGURE 2.1 Implied volatility surface of the S&P 500 as of July 18, 2012. Strikes are in percentage of the spot level.

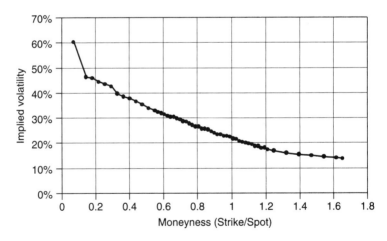

FIGURE 2.2 Implied volatility smile of S&P 500 index options expiring December 20, 2014, as of July 22, 2012.
Data source: Bloomberg.

parameter σ. We can see that the curve peaks at $\sigma \approx 30.8\%$ for a maximum price of $3.78. Thus, no single value of σ may reproduce any market price above $3.78. Interestingly, this phenomenon is not symmetric: $90–$100 put spreads can be priced with a single volatility parameter, but the value of σ will be significantly off the level of implied volatility for each put.

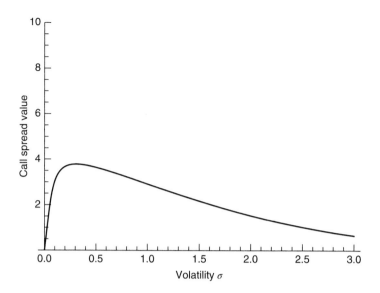

FIGURE 2.3 Black-Scholes value of a call spread as a function of volatility. Spot price $100, one-year maturity, strikes $100 and $110, zero rates and dividends.

2-1.2 Consequence for Hedge Ratios

The smile does not mean that Black-Scholes is wrong and should be rejected. Practitioners typically price over-the-counter (OTC) vanilla options using Black-Scholes and an appropriate volatility interpolation or extrapolation scheme, for the simple reason that implied volatilities are derived from listed option prices in the first place. In other words, the fact that the Black-Scholes model may be faulty is fairly irrelevant for vanilla option pricing.

However, the vanilla hedge ratios or Greeks are model-dependent and should be adjusted for the smile. To see this, notice first how a change in spot price impacts the moneyness of an option: after a $1 uptick from an initial $100 underlying spot price, an out-of-the-money call struck at $110 is now only $9 out of the money. In the presence of the smile, we may want to use a different implied volatility to reprice the call, and we must make an assumption on the behavior of the smile curve:

- If we assume that the smile curve does *not* change at all, we should use the same implied volatility to reprice the call. This is known as the sticky-strike rule and produces the same delta as Black-Scholes.
- If we assume that the smile curve does *not* change *with respect to* moneyness (strike over spot), we should use the implied volatility of the $110/101 \times 100 \approx \$108.91$ call to reprice the call. This is known as the sticky-moneyness rule and produces a higher delta than Black-Scholes.

- If we assume that the smile curve does *not* change *with respect to* delta, we should use the implied volatility corresponding to the new delta to reprice the call. This is known as the sticky-delta rule and produces a higher delta than Black-Scholes. Note that the consistent definition of delta is circular in this case.

Other rules would obviously produce different results.

FOCUS ON THE DELTA GENERATED BY THE SMILE

Assuming that the smile $\sigma^*(S, K, T)$ depends on spot, strike, and maturity, and denoting $c_{BS}(S, K, T, r, \sigma)$ the Black-Scholes formula for the European call, we have by the chain rule:

$$\delta = \frac{d}{dS} c_{BS}(S, K, T, r, \sigma^*(S, K, T)) = \frac{\partial c_{BS}}{\partial S} + \frac{\partial \sigma^*}{\partial S} \times \frac{\partial c_{BS}}{\partial \sigma} = \delta_{BS} + V_{BS} \times \frac{\partial \sigma^*}{\partial S}$$

where δ_{BS}, V_{BS} are the Black-Scholes delta and vega, respectively.

- In the sticky-strike rule we have $\frac{\partial \sigma^*}{\partial S} = 0$ and thus $\delta = \delta_{BS}$.
- In the sticky-moneyness rule we may rewrite $\sigma^*(S, K, T) \equiv \sigma_1^*\left(\frac{K}{S}, T\right)$ and thus $\delta = \delta_{BS} - V_{BS} \frac{K}{S^2} \frac{\partial \sigma_1^*}{\partial S}\left(\frac{K}{S}, T\right)$.
- To approach the sticky-delta rule we may rewrite $\sigma^*(S, K, T) \equiv \sigma_2^*\left(\ln \frac{K}{S}, T\right)$ since the Black-Scholes delta is $N(d_1) = N\left(\frac{\ln(S/K) + \left(r + \frac{1}{2}\sigma^2\right)T}{\sigma\sqrt{T}}\right)$ which is a function of $\ln(K/S)$. Thus $\delta = \delta_{BS} - V_{BS} \frac{1}{S} \frac{\partial \sigma_2^*}{\partial S}\left(\ln \frac{K}{S}, T\right)$.

2-1.3 Consequence for the Pricing of Exotics

In Chapter 3 we will see that European exotic payoffs can in theory be replicated by a static portfolio of vanilla options along a continuum of strikes. In the absence of arbitrage, the price of the exotic option must match the price of the portfolio. Thus it would be inaccurate to use the Black-Scholes model to price the exotic option in the presence of the smile.

As a fundamental example consider the digital option that pays off \$1 at maturity T if the final spot price S_T is above the strike K, and 0 otherwise.

The Black-Scholes value for the digital option is simply:

$$D_{BS}(S, K, r, T, \sigma) = e^{-rT}N(d_2) = e^{-rT}N\left(\frac{\ln(S/K) + \left(r - \frac{1}{2}\sigma^2\right)T}{\sigma\sqrt{T}}\right)$$

where S is the spot price, r is the continuous interest rate for maturity T, and σ is the constant Black-Scholes volatility parameter.

Digital options are difficult to delta-hedge because their delta becomes very large around the strike as maturity approaches. Equity exotic traders will typically overhedge them with tight call spreads. For example, to overhedge a digital paying off \$1,000,000 above a strike of \$100 and 0 otherwise, a trader might buy 200,000 call spreads with strikes \$95 and \$100.

Figure 2.4 shows how in general a quantity $1/\varepsilon$ of call spreads with strikes $K - \varepsilon$ and K will overhedge a digital option struck at K. In the limit as ε goes to zero, we obtain an exact hedging portfolio whose price is:

$$D(S, K, r, T) = D_{BS}(S, K, r, T, \sigma^*(K, T)) - V_{BS}(S, K, r, T, \sigma^*(K, T)) \times \frac{\partial\sigma^*}{\partial K}$$

where $\sigma^*(K, T)$ is the implied volatility for strike K and maturity T and V_{BS} is the Black-Scholes vega of a vanilla option. Because the equity smile is mostly downward-sloping we typically have $\frac{\partial\sigma^*}{\partial K} < 0$ and thus the digital option is worth more than its Black-Scholes value.

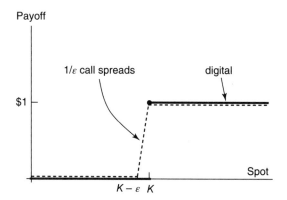

FIGURE 2.4 Digital and leveraged call spread payoffs.

2-2 INTERPOLATION AND EXTRAPOLATION

Implied volatilities derived from listed option prices are only available for a finite number of listed strikes and maturities. However, on the OTC market, option investors will ask for quotes for any strike or maturity, and it is important to be able to interpolate or extrapolate implied volatilities.

Interpolation is relatively easy: for a given maturity, if the at-the-money option has 20% implied volatility and the $90-strike option has 25% implied volatility, it intuitively makes sense to linearly interpolate and say that the $95-strike option should have a 22.5% implied volatility. Similarly, for a given strike, we can linearly interpolate implied volatility through time.

One issue with linear interpolation, however, is that it produces a cracked smile curve. More sophisticated interpolation techniques, such as cubic splines, are often used to obtain a smooth curve. Figure 2.5 compares the two methods.

It must be emphasized that unconstrained interpolation methods may produce arbitrageable volatility surfaces. Several papers listed in Homescu (2011) discuss how to eliminate arbitrage.

On the other hand extrapolation is a difficult endeavor: how to price a five-year option if the longest listed maturity is two years? There is no definite answer to this question, and we must typically resort to a volatility surface model (see Section 2-4).

Note that extrapolating a cubic spline fit tends to produce unpredictable results and should be avoided at all costs.

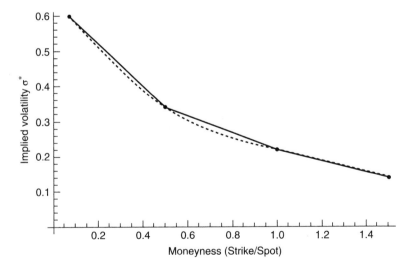

FIGURE 2.5 Comparison of linear (solid line) and cubic splines (dashed line) interpolation methods.

FOCUS ON CUBIC SPLINE INTERPOLATION

Given $n + 1$ points $(x_i, y_i)_{0 \leq i \leq n}$ we want to find a smooth function $S(x)$ that connects all the points. This may be done by defining n separate cubic polynomials for each interval $[x_i, x_{i+1}]$ where $i = 0, 1, \ldots, n - 1$ of the form:

$$S_i(x) = a_i(x - x_i)^3 + b_i(x - x_i)^2 + c_i(x - x_i) + d_i \quad \text{for } x_i \leq x \leq x_{i+1}$$

The spline interpolation function is the piecewise combination of the n functions $S_0, S_1, \ldots, S_{n-1}$:

$$S(x) = \begin{cases} S_0(x) & \text{if } x_0 \leq x \leq x_1 \\ S_1(x) & \text{if } x_1 \leq x \leq x_2 \\ \vdots & \vdots \\ S_{n-1}(x) & \text{if } x_{n-1} \leq x \leq x_n \end{cases}$$

There are thus $4n$ coefficients (a_i, b_i, c_i, d_i) to be chosen, for which we need $4n$ conditions. A first set of $2n$ conditions is provided by the requirement that $S(x)$ should connect all the points; that is: $S_i(x_i) = y_i$ and $S_i(x_{i+1}) = y_{i+1}$.

Another set of $2(n - 1)$ conditions is provided by requiring $S(x)$ to have continuous first- and second-order derivatives; that is: $S'_i(x_{i+1}) = S'_{i+1}(x_{i+1})$ and $S''_i(x_{i+1}) = S''_{i+1}(x_{i+1})$ for $i = 0, 1, \ldots, n - 2$.

This only leaves two additional conditions to be found in order to uniquely determine all coefficients (a_i, b_i, c_i, d_i). A common choice is to further require that $S''_0(x_0) = 0$ and $S''_{n-1}(x_n) = 0$.

Assuming for ease of exposure that all intervals are of unit length (i.e., $x_{i+1} - x_i = 1$), and rearranging all equations, we obtain $b_0 = 0$ and a beautiful tridiagonal linear system of the form:

$$\begin{bmatrix} 2 & 1 & & & & (0) \\ 1 & 4 & 1 & & & \\ & 1 & 4 & \ddots & & \\ & & 1 & \ddots & 1 & \\ & & & \ddots & 4 & 1 \\ (0) & & & & 1 & 2 \end{bmatrix} \begin{bmatrix} b_1 \\ b_2 \\ b_3 \\ \vdots \\ b_{n-2} \\ b_{n-1} \end{bmatrix} = 3 \begin{bmatrix} y_0 - 2y_1 + y_2 \\ y_1 - 2y_2 + y_3 \\ y_2 - 2y_3 + y_4 \\ \vdots \\ y_{n-3} - 2y_{n-2} + y_{n-1} \\ y_{n-2} - 2y_{n-1} + y_n \end{bmatrix}$$

The computation of the other coefficients is then straightforward.

2-3   IMPLIED VOLATILITY SURFACE PROPERTIES

Not every surface $f(K, T)$ is a candidate for an implied volatility surface $\sigma^*(K, T)$. Denote $c(S, K, T, r)$, $p(S, K, T, r)$ the call and put values induced by $\sigma^*(K, T)$, respectively. To preclude arbitrage we must at least require:

- No call or put spread arbitrage: $\dfrac{\partial c}{\partial K} \leq 0, \dfrac{\partial p}{\partial K} \geq 0$ (2.1)

- No butterfly spread arbitrage: $\dfrac{\partial^2 c}{\partial K^2} \geq 0, \dfrac{\partial^2 p}{\partial K^2} \geq 0$ (2.2)

- No calendar spread arbitrage[1]: $\dfrac{\partial c}{\partial T} \geq 0, \dfrac{\partial p}{\partial T} \geq 0$ (2.3)

These inequalities place upper and lower bounds on $\sigma^*(K, T)$ and its derivatives. For example, by the chain rule applied to $\frac{\partial c}{\partial K} = \frac{\partial}{\partial K} c_{BS}(S, K, T, r, \sigma^*(K, T))$, we obtain $\frac{\partial c}{\partial K} = \frac{\partial c_{BS}}{\partial K} + \frac{\partial c_{BS}}{\partial \sigma} \frac{\partial \sigma^*}{\partial K}$, and thus $\frac{\partial c}{\partial K} \leq 0$ is equivalent to the upper bound $\frac{\partial \sigma^*}{\partial K} \leq -\frac{\partial c_{BS}/\partial K}{\partial c_{BS}/\partial \sigma}\bigg|_{\sigma=\sigma^*(K,T)}$.

When designing an implied volatility surface model, it is important to check that these constraints are satisfied.

The implied volatility surface must also satisfy certain asymptotic properties. Perhaps the most notable one for fixed maturity is that implied variance, the square of implied volatility, is bounded from above by a function linear in log-strike as $k_F \to 0$ and $k_F \to \infty$:

$$\sigma^{*2}(k_F, T) \leq \beta T |\ln k_F|$$

where $k_F = K/F$ is the forward-moneyness and $\beta \in [0, 2]$ is different for each limit. This result is more rigorously expressed with supremum limits and we refer the interested reader to Lee (2004).

2-4   IMPLIED VOLATILITY SURFACE MODELS

Every large equity option house maintains several proprietary models of the implied volatility surface, which are used by their market-makers to mark positions. By definition these models are not in the public domain, and we must regrettably leave them in the dark. Fortunately some researchers have published their models and we now present a selection.

---

[1]For a given strike, American call and put prices must increase with maturity under penalty of arbitrage. This requirement is frequently extended to European option prices, although in theory small violations could be accepted.

There are two ways to model the volatility surface $\sigma^*(k, T)$:

1. Directly, by specifying a functional form such as a parametric function, or an interpolation and extrapolation method;
2. Indirectly, by modeling the behavior of the underlying asset differently from the geometric Brownian motion posited by Black-Scholes.

Here, it is worth distinguishing between two kinds of implied volatility σ^*: market-implied volatility σ^*_{Market}, which is computed from market prices; and model-implied volatility $\sigma^*_{[\text{Model}]}$, which is induced by a volatility surface model attempting to reproduce σ^*_{Market}. However, for ease of notation we will often keep the notation σ^* when there is no ambiguity nor need for such distinction.

2-4.1 A Parametric Model of Implied Volatility: The SVI Model

A popular parameterization of the smile for fixed maturity is the SVI model by Gatheral (2004). SVI stands for stochastic volatility-inspired and has the simple functional form:

$$\sigma^*_{\text{SVI}}(k_F, T) = \sqrt{a + b\left[\rho\left(\ln k_F - m\right) + \sqrt{(\ln k_F - m)^2 + s^2}\right]} \qquad (2.4)$$

where a, b, ρ, m, and s are parameters depending on T, and $k_F = K/F$ is the forward-moneyness. Intuitively a controls the overall level of variance, m corresponds to a moneyness shift, ρ is related to the correlation between stock prices and volatility and controls symmetry, s controls the smoothness near the money ($k_F = 1$), and b controls the angle between small and large strikes.

Figure 2.6 shows an example of the shape of the smile produced by the SVI model, which is plausible.

The SVI model is connected to stochastic volatility models (see Gatheral-Jacquier (2011)). Specifically, the authors show how Equation (2.4) is the limit-case of the implied volatility smile produced by the Heston model as the maturity goes to infinity.

To ensure the no-arbitrage condition Equation (2.1) we must have $b(1 + |\rho|) \leq \frac{4}{T}$. In his original 2004 talk, Gatheral claims that this condition is also sufficient to ensure Equation (2.2), but a recent report by Roper (2010) suggests otherwise.

An attractive property of the SVI model is that it is relatively easy to satisfy Equation (2.3) since its parameters are time dependent. This is also a drawback: as a surface, the SVI model has too many parameters.

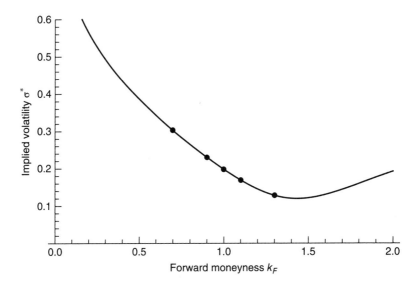

FIGURE 2.6 SVI fit of one-year implied volatility smile for the S&P 500 as of July 18, 2012. Black dots correspond to observed data.

To circumvent this issue, Gurrieri (2011) put forward a class of arbitrage-free SVI models with term structure using 11 time-homogenous parameters.

It should be noted that, being a function of $\ln \frac{K}{F}$ and thus $\ln \frac{K}{S}$, the SVI model incorporates the sticky-delta rule and thus produces a higher delta than Black-Scholes, as shown in Figure 2.7.

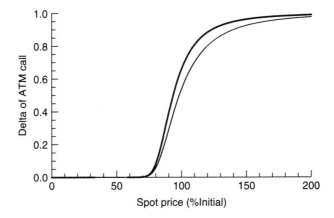

FIGURE 2.7 The SVI model of the implied volatility surface produces a higher delta than Black-Scholes.

FOCUS ON SVI MODEL FITTING

The classical approach to find model parameters is to perform a least square optimization against observed data. In the case of the SVI model, this means finding:

$$\min_{a,b,\rho,m,s} \sum_{i=1}^{n} \left[\sigma^{*2}_{\text{SVI}} \left(k_i, T; a, b, \rho, m, s \right) - \sigma^{*2}_{\text{Market}}(k_i, T) \right]^2$$

where T is a fixed listed maturity, $k_1, \ldots, k_n$ are n listed strikes in percentage of the forward price, and σ^*_{Market} is the implied volatility of the listed options observed on the market.

When solving numerically, it is often necessary to specify boundaries on the parameters: $a \geq 0, b \geq 0, -1 \leq \rho \leq 1, s > 0$. Additionally we may include the no-arbitrage constraint $b(1 + |\rho|)T \leq 4$. Note that while we could in principle let $a < 0$, this tends to generate bad results.

This will be enough for most optimization softwares. For faster computations, Zeliade Systems (2009) explains how the problem can be reduced to a two-dimensional optimization problem with nested linear program, for which there is a quasi-explicit solution.

2-4.2 Indirect Models of Implied Volatility

Any alternative to Black-Scholes will generate an implied volatility surface, which may be used to appraise the quality of the model. This is a major source of implied volatility surface models.

2-4.2.1 The SABR Model The stochastic alpha, beta, rho (SABR) model of Hagan and colleagues (2002) assumes that the underlying *forward price* dynamics are described by the coupled diffusion equations:

$$\begin{cases} dF_t = \sigma_t F_t^\beta dW_t \\ d\sigma_t = \alpha \sigma_t dZ_t \end{cases}$$

where W and Z are standard Brownian motions with $(dW_t)(dZ_t) \equiv \rho dt$ and α, β, ρ are constant model parameters.

In the special case $\beta = 1$ an analytical formula for implied volatility is available for short maturities, which allows to fit the parameters to observed option prices. Near the money the formula has the Taylor expansion expression:

$$\sigma_{\text{SABR}}^*(k, T) \underset{\substack{T \to 0 \\ k \to 1}}{\approx} \sigma_0 \left[1 + \frac{1}{2}\rho\frac{\alpha \ln k}{\sigma_0} + \frac{2 - 3\rho^2}{12}\left(\frac{\alpha \ln k}{\sigma_0}\right)^2 \right.$$
$$\left. + \left(\frac{1}{4}\rho\sigma_0\alpha + \frac{2 - 3\rho^2}{12}\frac{\alpha^2}{2}\right) T \right]$$

The SABR model is popular for interest rates where the smile is more symmetric than for equities.

2-4.2.2 The Heston Model The Heston (1993) model is perhaps the most popular approach for stochastic volatility. It assumes the following underlying spot price dynamics coupled to an instantaneous variance process:

$$\begin{cases} dS_t = \mu_t S_t dt + \sqrt{v_t}S_t dW_t \\ dv_t = \kappa\left(\bar{v} - v_t\right) dt + \omega\sqrt{v_t}dZ_t \end{cases}$$

where W and Z are standard Brownian motions with $(dW_t)(dZ_t) \equiv \rho dt$ and $\kappa, \bar{v}, \omega, \rho$ are constant model parameters that must satisfy the Feller condition $2\kappa\bar{v} \geq \omega^2$ to ensure strictly positive instantaneous variance v_t at all times. The instantaneous rate of return μ_t on the underlying asset can be anything since it will disappear under the risk-neutral measure.

Rouah (2013) provides a valuable resource detailing the theoretical and practical aspects of the Heston model, including code examples.

Although no analytical formula for implied volatility is available, the popularity of the Heston model is largely due to the existence of quasi-analytical formulas for European options making the computation of implied volatilities very quick.

Figure 2.8 compares a Heston fit to the S&P 500 implied volatility surface. We can see that the Heston model produces a plausible shape but is too flat for short expiries.

One limitation of the Heston model is that instantaneous variance is a somewhat elusive concept, which cannot be measured in practice. However an analytical formula for the total expected variance over a period $[0, T]$ is available:

$$\mathbb{E}\left(\int_0^T v_t dt\right) = \bar{v}T + \frac{1}{\kappa}(1 - e^{-\kappa T})(v_0 - \bar{v}) \approx v_0 T$$

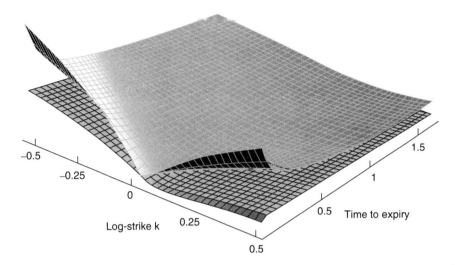

FIGURE 2.8 Comparison of the S&P 500 implied volatility surface (top) with its Heston fit (bottom) as of September 15, 2005.
Source: Jim Gatheral, *The Implied Volatility Surface: A Practitioner's Guide* (Hoboken, NJ: John Wiley & Sons, 2005). Reprinted with permission of John Wiley & Sons, Inc.

Hence the expected total annualized variance is approximately constant at v_0 regardless of maturity, which is inconsistent with empirical market observations (see Section 5-2).

FOCUS ON THE FELLER CONDITION

Diffusion processes of the form $dX_t = a_t dt + b_t dW_t$ may a priori span the entire real line $(-\infty, +\infty)$. However, we know that the geometric Brownian motion obtained with $a_t = \mu X_t, b_t = \sigma X_t$ remains strictly positive if $X_0 > 0$. When modeling quantities such as stock prices, interest rates, or instantaneous variance, it is often useful to ensure that these quantities remain bounded between certain levels ℓ and u (possibly infinite). This will be the case when the coefficients a_t, b_t satisfy certain conditions.

First, observe that if a_t, b_t depend on X_t and take the value 0 at ℓ and u the process is automatically bounded by $[\ell, u]$ by continuity of diffusion paths. This is a useful sufficient condition for boundedness but it is by no means necessary.

The lower boundary ℓ is then classified as:

- Attracting if, starting from x above ℓ, the process (X_t) may hit ℓ before an arbitrary level $b > x$ with positive probability
- Non-attracting otherwise

The same classification applies to the upper boundary u through a symmetric definition. Note that the hitting time could be infinite, which calls for a further distinction between attainable and unattainable attracting boundaries. We refer the interested reader to Karlin and Taylor (1981).

When the diffusion is time-homogeneous with drift and volatility coefficients $a(x), b(x)$; that is, (X_t) is of the form $dX_t = a(X_t)dt + b(X_t)dW_t$, a characterization for the lower boundary ℓ to be non-attracting is:

$$\lim_{x \downarrow \ell} \int_x^{x_0} s(y)dy = \infty \quad s(y) = \exp\left(-\int_{y_0}^y \frac{2a(x)}{b^2(x)}dx\right)$$

where x_0 and y_0 are arbitrary fixed points inside (ℓ, u).

We now derive the corresponding Feller condition at $\ell = 0$ for the process $dX_t = \kappa(\theta - X_t)dt + \omega\sqrt{X_t}dW_t$ so that the values remain in $(0, \infty)$. Substituting the drift and volatility coefficients in the definition of $s(y)$ we have:

$$s(y) = \exp\left(-\int_{y_0}^y \frac{2\kappa(\theta - x)}{\omega^2 x}dx\right) = \left(\frac{y_0}{y}\right)^{2\frac{\kappa\theta}{\omega^2}} e^{\frac{2\kappa}{\omega^2}(y - y_0)}$$

Since $\lim_{y \to 0} e^{\frac{2\kappa}{\omega^2}(y - y_0)} = e^{-\frac{2\kappa}{\omega^2}y_0} > 0$ the improper integral $\int_0^{x_0} s(y)dy$ will diverge if and only if $2\frac{\kappa\theta}{\omega^2} \geq 1$, which is the Feller condition for the Heston model.

2-4.2.3 The LNV Model Recently Carr and Wu (2011) proposed a sophisticated framework for the underlying forward price dynamics, which results in a closed-form formula for implied volatility. The forward price process solves the diffusion equation:

$$dF_t = \sqrt{v_t}F_t dW_t$$

where W is a standard Brownian motion and v is an arbitrary stochastic instantaneous variance process. Furthermore, the entire implied volatility surface $\sigma_t^*(K, T)$ is assumed to evolve through time according to the diffusion equation:

$$d\sigma_t^*(K, T) = \mu_t(K, T)dt + \omega_t(K, T)dZ_t$$

where Z is a standard Brownian motion with $(dW_t)(dZ_t) \equiv \rho_t dt$ and μ, ω, ρ may be stochastic.

Carr-Wu then show that in this setup the implied volatility surface at any time t is fully determined by a quadratic equation, which depends on μ_t, ω_t, ρ_t and the unspecified v_t.

This very general framework can produce a wide range of implied volatility surfaces. Choosing $\mu_t = \kappa(\theta - \sigma_t^{*2}(K, T))$ and $\omega_t = we^{-\eta(T-t)}\sigma_t^{*2}(K, T)$ yields the Log-Normal Variance (LNV) model in which $\sigma_{LNV,0}^{*2}(k, T)$ is solution to the quadratic equation:

$$\frac{w^2}{4}e^{-2\eta T}\sigma_{LNV,0}^{*4}(k, T) + [1 + \kappa T + w^2 e^{-2\eta T}T - \rho w \sqrt{v}e^{-\eta T}T]\sigma_{LNV,0}^{*2}(k, T)$$

$$- [v + \kappa\theta\tau + 2w\rho\sqrt{v}e^{-\eta T}\ln k + w^2 e^{-2\eta T}\ln^2 k] = 0$$

where $\kappa, w, \eta, \theta, v, \rho$ are constant parameters and k denotes moneyness K/S_0.

The LNV model thus combines two attractive features: a functional parametric form for the implied volatility, and known dynamics for the evolution of the underlying spot price as well as the implied volatility surface itself.

REFERENCES AND BIBLIOGRAPHY

Carr, Peter, and Liuren Wu. 2011. "A New Simple Approach for Constructing Implied Volatility Surfaces." Working paper, New York University and Baruch College.

Derman, Emanuel. 2010. "Introduction to the Volatility Smile." Lecture notes, Columbia University.

Gatheral, Jim. 2004. "A Parsimonious Arbitrage-Free Implied Volatility Parameterization with Application to the Valuation of Volatility Derivatives." Proceedings of the Global Derivatives and Risk Management 2004 Madrid conference.

Gatheral, Jim. 2005. *The Implied Volatility Surface: A Practitioner's Guide*. Hoboken, NJ: John Wiley & Sons.

Gatheral, Jim, and Antoine Jacquier. 2011. "Convergence of Heston to SVI." *Quantitative Finance* 11 (8): 1129–1132.

Gurrieri, Sébastien. 2011. "A Class of Term Structures for SVI Implied Volatility." Working paper. Available at http://ssrn.com/abstract=1779463 or http://dx.doi.org/10.2139/ssrn.1779463.

Hagan, Patrick S., Deep Kumar, Andrew L. Lesniewski, and Diana E. Woodward. 2002. "Managing Smile Risk." *Wilmott Magazine* (September): 84–108.

Heston, Stephen L. 1993. "A Closed-Form Solution for Options with Stochastic Volatility with Applications to Bond and Currency Options." *Review of Financial Studies* 6 (2): 327–343.

Hodges, Hardy M. 1996. "Arbitrage Bounds on the Implied Volatility Strike and Term Structures of European-Style Options." *Journal of Derivatives* (Summer): 23–35.

Homescu, Cristian. 2011. "Implied Volatility Surface: Construction Methodologies and Characteristics." Available at http://arxiv.org/abs/1107.1834v1.

Karlin, Samuel, and Howard M. Taylor. 1981. "Diffusion Processes." In *A Second Course in Stochastic Processes*, 157–396. San Diego, CA: Academic Press.

Lee, Roger. 2004. "The Moment Formula for Implied Volatility at Extreme Strikes." *Mathematical Finance* 14: 469–480.

Roper, Michael. 2010. "Arbitrage Free Implied Volatility Surfaces." Working paper. Available at www.maths.usyd.edu.au/u/pubs/publist/preprints/2010/roper-9 .pdf.

Rouah, Fabrice. 2013. *The Heston Model in Matlab and C#*. Hoboken, NJ: John Wiley & Sons.

Zeliade Systems. 2009. "Quasi-Explicit Calibration of Gatheral's SVI model." Zeliade White Paper.

PROBLEMS

2.1   No Call or Put Spread Arbitrage Condition

Consider an underlying asset S with spot price S and forward price F. Let r denote the continuous interest rate for maturity T, $U(S, K, T, r)$, $L(S, K, T, r)$ be the upper and lower bounds on the slope of the smile corresponding to the no call or put spread arbitrage condition (2.1). Given $\frac{\partial c_{BS}}{\partial K} = -e^{-rT}N(d_2)$, $\frac{\partial c_{BS}}{\partial \sigma} = Ke^{-rT}\sqrt{T}N'(d_2)$, show that that $U - L = \frac{\sqrt{2\pi}\exp(d_1^2)}{F\sqrt{T}}$ where $d_{1,2} = \frac{\ln(F/K) \pm \frac{1}{2}\sigma^{*2}T}{\sigma^*\sqrt{T}}$.

2.2   No Butterfly Spread Arbitrage Condition

Assume zero interest rates and dividends. Consider the Black-Scholes formula for the European call struck at K with maturity T:

$$C(S, K, T, \sigma) = SN(d_1) - KN(d_2) \quad d_{1,2} = \frac{\ln(S/K) \pm \frac{1}{2}\sigma^2 T}{\sigma\sqrt{T}}$$

where S is the underlying asset's spot price, σ is the volatility parameter, and $N(.)$ is the cumulative distribution function of a standard normal.

(a) Given $\frac{\partial C}{\partial K} = -N(d_2)$, $\frac{\partial C}{\partial \sigma} = K\sqrt{T}N'(d_2)$, derive the identities:

- $$\frac{\partial^2 C}{\partial K^2} = \frac{N'(d_2)}{K\sigma\sqrt{T}}$$

- $$\frac{\partial^2 C}{\partial \sigma \partial K} = \frac{d_1}{\sigma}N'(d_2)$$

- $$\frac{\partial^2 C}{\partial \sigma^2} = \frac{d_1 d_2}{\sigma}K\sqrt{T}N'(d_2)$$

(b) *A second-order chain rule.* Show that if $f(x, y)$ and $u(t)$ are C^2 (twice continuously differentiable) then the second-order derivative of $\varphi(t) = f(t, u(t))$ is given as:

$$\varphi'' = f_{xx} + 2 u' f_{xy} + u'^2 f_{yy} + u'' f_y, \text{ i.e.:}$$

$$\varphi''(t) = f_{xx}[t, u(t)] + 2u'(t) f_{xy}[t, u(t)] + (u'(t))^2 f_{yy}[t, u(t)] + u''(t) f_y[t, u(t)]$$

where f_{xx}, f_{xy}, and f_{yy} denote the second-order partial derivatives of f.

(c) Assume that the implied volatility smile $\sigma^*(K)$ is C^2 for a given maturity T. Using your results in (a) and (b), show that for $c(S, K, T) = C(S, K, T, \sigma^*(K))$:

$$\frac{\partial^2 c}{\partial K^2} = \frac{N'(d_2)}{K\sigma^*(K)\sqrt{T}} \left[1 + 2d_1 \left(K\sigma^{*\prime}(K)\sqrt{T} \right) + d_1 d_2 \left(K\sigma^{*\prime}(K)\sqrt{T} \right)^2 \right.$$

$$\left. + \left(K\sigma^{*\prime\prime}(K)\sqrt{T} \right) (K\sigma^*(K)\sqrt{T}) \right]$$

(d) What does the no butterfly arbitrage condition (2.2) reduce to?

2.3 Sticky True Delta Rule

Consider a one-year vanilla call with strike $K = 1$, and let $\sigma^*(S)$ be its implied volatility at various spot price assumptions S. Assume zero rates and dividends and denote the call price:

$$c(S) = c_{BS}(S, \sigma^*(S)) = SN\left(\frac{\ln S + \frac{1}{2}\sigma^{*2}(S)}{\sigma^*(S)} \right) - N\left(\frac{\ln S - \frac{1}{2}\sigma^{*2}(S)}{\sigma^*(S)} \right)$$

(a) Show that the option's delta Δ is

$$\Delta(S) = \frac{dc}{dS} = N\left(\frac{\ln S + \frac{1}{2}\sigma^{*2}(S)}{\sigma^*(S)}\right) + \sigma^{*\prime}(S)N'\left(\frac{\ln S - \frac{1}{2}\sigma^{*2}(S)}{\sigma^*(S)}\right)$$

(b) Assume that σ^* is a linear function of Δ: $\sigma^*(S) = a + b\Delta(S)$. Show that Δ is solution to the first-order differential equation:

$$\Delta = N\left(\frac{\ln S + \frac{1}{2}(a + b\Delta)^2}{a + b\Delta}\right) + bN'\left(\frac{\ln S - \frac{1}{2}(a + b\Delta)^2}{a + b\Delta}\right)\Delta'$$

(c) Is Δ higher or lower than the Black-Scholes delta?

2.4 SVI Fit

Using your favorite optimization software (Matlab, Mathematica, etc.) find the parameters for the SVI model corresponding to a least square fit of the following one-year implied volatility data:

Strike (%forward)	20%	50%	70%	90%	100%	110%	130%	150%	160%
Implied volatility	45.5%	34.6%	29.4%	24.0%	22.3%	19.9%	16.4%	14.9%	14.3%

Answer: $a = 0.0180$, $b = 0.0516$, $\rho = -0.9443$, $m = 0.2960$, $s = 0.1350$ using initial condition $a = 0.04$, $b = 0.4$, $\rho = -0.4$, $m = 0.05$, $s = 0.1$, and bounds $a > 0$, $0 < b < 2$, $-1 < \rho < 1$, $s > 0$.

CHAPTER 3

Implied Distributions

Perhaps the favorite activity of quantitative analysts is to decode market data into information about the future upon which a trader can base his or her decisions. This is the purpose of the implied distribution that translates option prices into probabilities for the underlying stock or stock index to reach certain levels in the future. In this chapter, we derive the implied distribution and show how it may be exploited to price and hedge certain exotic payoffs.

3-1 BUTTERFLY SPREADS AND THE IMPLIED DISTRIBUTION

Vanilla option prices contain probability information about the market's guess at the future level of the underlying asset S. For example, suppose that Kroger Co. trades at $24 and that one-year calls struck at $24 and $25 trade at $1 and $0.60 respectively. If interest rates are zero, we may then infer that the probability of the terminal spot price S_T in one year to be above $24 must satisfy:

$$\mathbb{P}\{S_T > 24\} = \mathbb{E}(I_{\{S_T>24\}})$$
$$\geq 1 - 0.6 = 0.4,$$

because the digital payoff $I_{\{S_T>24\}}$ dominates the call spread as shown in Figure 3.1.

Similarly the price of a butterfly spread with strikes $23, $24, and $25 (i.e., long one call struck at $23, short two calls struck at $24, and long one call struck at $25) will give a lower bound for $\mathbb{P}\{23 < S_T < 25\}$ as shown in Figure 3.2.

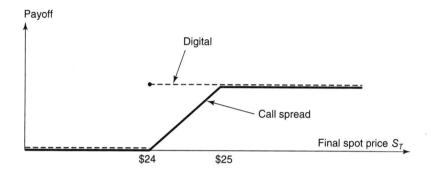

FIGURE 3.1 The digital payoff dominates the call spread payoff.

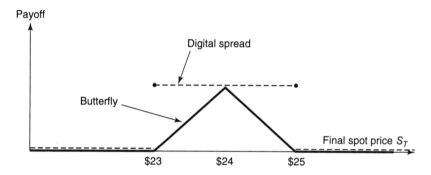

FIGURE 3.2 The digital spread payoff dominates the butterfly spread payoff.

Generally, if all option prices are available along a continuum of strikes—such as option prices generated by an implied volatility surface model—we may consider butterfly spreads with strikes $K - \varepsilon, K, K + \varepsilon$ leveraged by $1/\varepsilon^2$ and obtain in the limit as $\varepsilon \to 0$ the **implied distribution density** of S_T:

$$\mathbb{P}\{S_T = K\} = e^{rT} \lim_{\varepsilon \to 0} \frac{c(K - \varepsilon) - 2c(K) + c(K + \varepsilon)}{\varepsilon^2} = e^{rT} \frac{d^2 c}{dK^2} \qquad (3.1)$$

where r is the continuous interest rate for maturity T, and $c(K)$ denotes the price of the call struck at K.

Note that by put-call parity we have $\frac{d^2 c}{dK^2} = \frac{d^2 p}{dK^2}$ and thus put prices may alternatively be used to compute the implied distribution density.

Figure 3.3 compares the Black-Scholes lognormal density to the implied distribution density generated by an SVI model fit of S&P 500 option prices with about 2.4-year maturity. We can see that the implied density is skewed toward the right and has a fatter left tail.

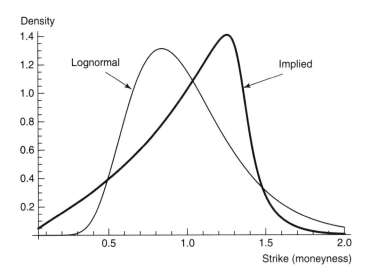

FIGURE 3.3 The lognormal and implied distribution densities.

The implied distribution density may be obtained directly from a smooth volatility surface $\sigma^*(K, T)$ by differentiating $c(K) = c_{BS}(S, K, T, r, \sigma^*(K, T))$ twice with respect to K (see Problem 2.2 (c)). The corresponding formula is:

$$\mathbb{P}\{S_T = K\} = \frac{N'(d_2)}{K\sigma^*\sqrt{T}} \left[1 + 2d_1 \left(K\frac{\partial\sigma^*}{\partial K}\sqrt{T} \right) + d_1 d_2 \left(K\frac{\partial\sigma^*}{\partial K}\sqrt{T} \right)^2 \right.$$
$$\left. + \left(K\frac{\partial^2\sigma^*}{\partial K^2}\sqrt{T} \right)(K\sigma^*\sqrt{T}) \right] \qquad (3.2)$$

where $d_{1,2} = \frac{\ln(F/K) \pm \frac{1}{2}\sigma^{*2}T}{\sigma^*\sqrt{T}}$, F is the forward price of S for maturity T, and $N'(\cdot)$ is the standard normal distribution density. It is worth emphasizing that Equation (3.2) relies on partial derivatives of σ^* with respect to the dollar strike K, and that one must be careful when using an implied volatility model such as the SVI model, which is based on forward-moneyness $k_F = K/F$. In the latter case, we must substitute $\frac{\partial\sigma^*}{\partial K} = \frac{1}{F} \times \frac{\partial\sigma^*_{SVI}}{\partial k_F}$ and $\frac{\partial^2\sigma^*}{\partial K^2} = \frac{1}{F^2} \times \frac{\partial^2\sigma^*_{SVI}}{\partial k_F^2}$.

The first factor, $\frac{N'(d_2)}{K\sigma^*\sqrt{T}}$, is the Black-Scholes lognormal distribution at point K using implied volatility. Without the second factor between brackets, the integral does not sum to 1, unless the smile is flat.

The implied distribution reveals what options markets "think" in terms of the future evolution of the underlying asset price. It is a useful theoretical concept, but in practice it can be difficult to exploit this information for trading.

3-2   EUROPEAN PAYOFF PRICING AND REPLICATION

Consider an option with arbitrary European payoff $f(S_T)$ at maturity T, and let $h(K) = \mathbb{P}\{S_T = K\}$ be the implied distribution density. The corresponding option value is then $f_0 = e^{-rT}\mathbb{E}(f(S_T)) = e^{-rT}\int_0^\infty f(K)h(K)dK$ and by direct substitution of Equation (3.1) we obtain the Breeden-Litzenberger (1978) formula:

$$f_0 = \int_0^\infty f(K)\frac{d^2c}{dK^2}dK$$

The knowledge of the implied distribution thus allows us to value any European option consistently with the vanilla option market. It turns out that this value is in fact an arbitrage price, at least in theory when we can trade all vanilla options along a continuum of strikes $K > 0$.

To see this, assume that f is bounded and smooth (twice continuously differentiable) to perform an integration by parts and write:

$$f_0 = \int_0^\infty f(K)c''(K)dK = [f(K)c'(K)]_0^\infty - \int_0^\infty f'(K)c'(K)dK$$

$$= -f(0)c'(0) - \int_0^\infty f'(K)c'(K)dK$$

because infinite-strike calls are worthless. Integrating by parts again yields:

$$f_0 = -f(0)c'(0) + f'(0)c(0) + \int_0^\infty f''(K)c(K)dK$$

Furthermore zero-strike calls are always worth $c(0) = e^{-rT}F$; additionally, by put-call parity $c(K) = p(K) + e^{-rT}(F - K)$, thus by differentiation $c'(K) = p'(K) - e^{-rT}$ and since zero-strike puts are worthless we have $c'(0) = -e^{-rT}$. Substituting into the previous equation we get:

$$f_0 = f(0)e^{-rT} + f'(0)Fe^{-rT} + \int_0^\infty f''(K)c(K)dK$$

This expression suggests that the option may be hedged with a portfolio:

- Long zero-coupon bonds in quantity $f(0)e^{-rT}$
- Long zero-strike calls in quantity $f'(0)$
- Long all vanilla calls struck at $K > 0$ in quantities $f''(K)dK$

The definite proof of this result is provided by establishing that the option payoff perfectly matches the portfolio payoff:

$$f(S_T) = f(0) + f'(0)S_T + \int_0^\infty f''(K) \max(0, S_T - K) dK$$

which simply turns out to be the first-order Taylor expansion of f over $[0, S_T]$ with remainder in integral form after noticing that the bounds of the integral are actually 0 and S_T.

An alternative approach mixing puts and calls is developed in Problem 3.2.

This is a strong fundamental result that directs how to price and hedge European payoffs, with the following limitations:

- It only applies to European payoffs. Other option payoffs that depend on the history of the underlying asset price (such as Asian or barrier options) or have an early exercise feature (such as American options) require more sophisticated valuation methods and cannot be perfectly replicated with a static portfolio of vanilla options.
- In practice, only a finite number of strikes are available. While it is possible to overhedge convex payoffs with a finite portfolio of vanillas, exact replication cannot be achieved.

FOCUS ON OVERHEDGING

Exotic option traders often look at ways to overhedge a particular option payoff with a portfolio of vanillas, and price it accordingly. They will then underwrite the exotic option and buy the vanilla portfolio on the option market; at maturity, any difference in value will be a positive profit.

Consider for example the exotic option payoff $f(S_T) = \min\left(1, \frac{S_T^2}{S_0^2}\right)$ ("capped quadratic"). Using the implied distribution shown in Figure 3.3 we find a theoretical price of 79%.

The following are two possible overhedging strategies:

- An at-the-money covered call (i.e., long one stock and short an at-the-money call). The cost of this strategy is $1 - c(1) \approx 87\%$, which is significantly more expensive than the theoretical price.
- Long 1/2 stock, long one call struck at 50%, short 1.5 at-the-money calls. The cost of this strategy is $1/2 + c(0.5) - 1.5 \times c(1) \approx 81\%$, which is much closer to the theoretical price.

Figure 3.4 compares the payoffs of the exotic option versus the two overhedging portfolios.

Following the methodology of Demeterfi, Derman, Kamal, and Zhou (1999), in general any convex portion of a payoff $f(S_T)$ over

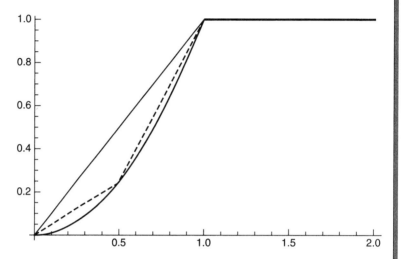

FIGURE 3.4 Payoffs of an exotic option and two possible vanilla overhedges.

an interval $[S_-, S_+]$ may be overhedged using, for example, n vanilla calls struck at $S_- = K_1 < K_2 < \cdots < K_n < S_+$ in quantities $q_1, \ldots, q_n$ and zero-coupon bonds in quantity $e^{-rT}f(S_-)$ such that:

$$
\begin{cases}
f(S_-) + \displaystyle\sum_{i=1}^{n-1} q_i \max(0, K_j - K_i) = f(K_j) \text{ for all } 2 \leq j \leq n \\
f(S_-) + \displaystyle\sum_{i=1}^{n} q_i \max(0, S_+ - K_i) = f(S_+)
\end{cases}
$$

We may then bootstrap the quantities q_i as follows:

$$
q_1 = \frac{f(K_2) - f(K_1)}{K_2 - K_1}
$$

$$
q_2 = \frac{f(K_3) - f(K_2)}{K_3 - K_2} - q_1
$$

$$
\vdots
$$

$$
q_n = \frac{f(S_+) - f(K_n)}{S_+ - K_n} - \sum_{i=1}^{n-1} q_i
$$

In our capped quadratic option example over $[0, 1]$ with strikes spaced 0.25 apart, we find quantities $q_1 = 0.25$ and $q_2 = q_3 = q_4 = 0.5$, and the convex portion of the portfolio payoff is very close to the actual payoff as shown in Figure 3.5.

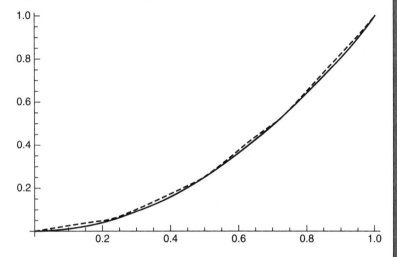

FIGURE 3.5 Overhedging the "capped quadratic" option with calls.

3-3 PRICING METHODS FOR EUROPEAN PAYOFFS

As stated earlier, the implied distribution $h(K) = \mathbb{P}\{S_T = K\}$ makes it possible to price any European payoff $f(S_T)$. Several numerical integration methods, such as the trapezoidal method, are then available to compute $f_0 = e^{-rT} \int_0^\infty f(K)h(K)dK$. One issue is that these methods become inefficient in large dimensions (i.e., multi-asset payoffs), which is the topic of Chapters 6 to 9.

Another approach is Monte Carlo simulation, which is easy to generalize to multiple dimensions. Using a cutoff $A \gg 0$ we may approximate f_0 by:

$$f_0 \approx e^{-rT} \int_0^A f(u)h(u)du \approx \frac{e^{-rT}}{nA} \sum_{i=1}^n f(Au_i)h(Au_i)$$

where $u_1, \ldots, u_n$ are n independent simulations from a uniform distribution over $[0, 1]$.

We can improve this approach by means of the **importance sampling** technique, which exploits the fact that the implied distribution is bell-shaped and somewhat similar to the Black-Scholes lognormal distribution $\ell(K) = \frac{1}{K\sigma\sqrt{T}}N'(d_2)$ with sensible volatility parameter σ (e.g., at-the-money implied volatility for maturity T). To do so, rewrite:

$$f_0 = e^{-rT}\int_0^\infty f(u)\frac{h(u)}{\ell(u)}\ell(u)du = e^{-rT}\mathbb{E}\left[f(X)\frac{h(X)}{\ell(X)}\right] \approx \frac{e^{-rT}}{n}\sum_{i=1}^n f(x_i)\frac{h(x_i)}{\ell(x_i)}$$

where X is lognormally distributed with density $\ell(K)$ and $x_1, \ldots, x_n$ are simulated values of X. The ratio $h(X)/\ell(X)$ measures how close the implied and lognormal distributions are.

Simulating X is straightforward through the identity $X = F \times \exp\left(\tilde{\varepsilon}\sigma\sqrt{T} - \frac{1}{2}\sigma^2 T\right)$ where $\tilde{\varepsilon}$ is a standard normal, for which there are many efficient pseudo-random generators. For completeness we provide the Matlab code to price the "capped quadratic" payoff according to the implied distribution shown in Figure 3.3.

```
function price = ImpDistMC(n)
  %Note: this algorithm assumes zero rates and dividends

  epsilon = 0.0001;

  T = 2.41; %maturity

  function val = Payoff(S)
    val = min(1, S^2);
  end

  function vol = SVI(k)
    a = 0.02;
    b = 0.05;
    rho = -1;
    m = 0.3;
    s = 0.1;

    k = log(k);
    vol = sqrt( a + b*( rho*(k-m) + sqrt( (k-m)^2 + s^2 ) ) );
  end

  function density = ImpDist(k)
    vol = SVI(k);
    volPrime = (SVI(k+epsilon)-vol)/epsilon;
                  %finite difference

    volDblPrime = (SVI(k+epsilon)-2*vol+SVI(k-epsilon))/epsilon^2;
                  %finite diff.

    d1 = (-log(k)+0.5*vol^2*T)/(vol*sqrt(T));
```

```
d2 = d1 - vol*sqrt(T);

density = normpdf(d2)/(k*vol*sqrt(T)) * (1 + ...
          2*d1*k*volPrime*sqrt(T) + ...
          d1*d2*(k*volPrime*sqrt(T))^2 + ...
          (k*volDblPrime*sqrt(T))*(k*vol*sqrt(T)) );
end


%%%%%%%%%%%%%%%%%%%%%%%%%%%%
%%% MAIN FUNCTION BODY %%%
%%%%%%%%%%%%%%%%%%%%%%%%%%%%

atm_vol = SVI(1);

price = 0;
for i=1:n
  x = exp(atm_vol*randn*sqrt(T) - 0.5*atm_vol^2*T);
     %lognormal simulation

  price = (i-1)/i*price + Payoff(x)*ImpDist(x) ...
        / lognpdf(x,-0.5*atm_vol^2*T,atm_vol*sqrt(T)) / i;
end
end
```

3-4 GREEKS

Because the implied distribution is derived from vanilla option prices in the first place, it produces the same delta as the input volatility smile. Consequently, if the implied volatility smile incorporates a sticky-delta rule, the delta obtained by repricing calls using the implied distribution will be higher than the Black-Scholes delta.

The implied distribution also makes it possible to calculate smile-consistent Greeks for any European payoff. In practice this is often done using finite differences, but one must be careful with the numerical precision of the method used for pricing. In particular the Monte Carlo method has error of order $1/\sqrt{n}$ where n is the number of simulations, and will generate a different price on each call unless the pseudo-random generator is systematically initialized at the same seed.

It is worth emphasizing that the implied distribution depends on the variables or parameters used for the Greeks. For example, if the payoff $f(S_T)$ is independent from the initial spot price S_0 the delta may be written $\frac{\partial f_0}{\partial S_0} = e^{-rT} \int_0^\infty f(x) \frac{\partial}{\partial S_0} \mathbb{P}\{S_T = x\} dx$ which involves the derivative of the implied distribution with respect to the spot price.

REFERENCES

Breeden, Douglas T., and Robert H. Litzenberger. 1978. "Prices of State-Contingent Claims Implicit in Option Prices." *Journal of Business* 51 (4): 621–651.

Demeterfi, Kresimir, Emanuel Derman, Michael Kamal, and Joseph Zhou. 1999. "More than You Ever Wanted to Know about Volatility Swaps." *Goldman Sachs Quantitative Strategies Research Notes*, March.

PROBLEMS

3.1 Overhedging Concave Payoffs

Consider a concave payoff $f(S_T)$ over an interval $[S_-, S_+]$. Propose a method to overhedge this payoff using a finite portfolio of vanilla calls.

3.2 Perfect Hedging with Puts and Calls

Show that for any smooth (twice continuously differentiable) payoff $f(S_T)$:

$$f(S_T) = \alpha + \beta S_T + \int_0^F f''(K) \max(0, K - S_T) dK$$
$$+ \int_F^\infty f''(K) \max(0, S_T - K) dK$$

where F is the forward price and α and β are constants to be identified. What is the corresponding option price f_0?

3.3 Implied Distribution and Exotic Pricing

(a) Reproduce Figure 3.3 using $T = 2.4$ and the following parameters for the SVI model: $a = 0.02$, $b = 0.05$, $\rho = -1$, $m = 0.3$, $s = 0.1$. Assume $S_0 = 1$ as well as zero interest and dividend rates.

(b) Using a numerical integration algorithm check the price of the "capped quadratic" option, then compute the price of the following option payoffs:

- $f(S_T) = \max\left(0, \dfrac{S_T - 1}{S_T}\right)$

- $f(S_T) = \begin{cases} \max\left(1 + C, \sqrt{S_T}\right) & \text{if } S_T > 75\% \\ S_T & \text{otherwise} \end{cases}$, where $C = 25\%$. Then solve for C to obtain a price of 100%.
- $f(S_T) = -\frac{2}{T} \ln S_T$. What is $\sqrt{f_0}$?
- $f(S_T) = \max(0, (S_T - 1)^3)$. Then find a vanilla overhedge over the interval $[0,2]$ with strikes 0.5, 0.9, 1, 1.1, 1.3, 1.7 and compare the price of the overhedge with the theoretical price.

3.4 Conditional Pricing

On August 24, 2012, Kroger Co.'s stock traded at $21.795, and options maturing in 511 days had the following implied volatilities:

Strike (%Spot)	30%	50%	70%	90%	100%	110%	130%	150%	200%
Impl. Vol. (%)	49.58	36.59	30.17	25.43	24.23	22.97	21.40	20.86	22.89

The forward price was $21.366, and the continuous interest rate was 0.81%.

(a) Calibrate the SVI model parameters to this data. *Answer: $a = 0$, $b = 0.1272$, $\rho = -0.7249$, $m = -0.1569$, $s = 0.5388$ using initial condition $a = 0.04$, $b = 0.4$, $\rho = -0.4$, $m = 0.05$, $s = 0.1$, and bounds $a > 0$, $0 < b < 2.024$, $-1 < \rho < 1$, $s > 0$.*

(b) Produce the graph of the corresponding implied distribution and compute the price of the "capped quadratic" option with payoff $f(S_T) = \min(1, (S_T/S_0)^2)$ using the numerical method of your choice. *Answer: approximately $0.797.*

(c) The following graph (Figure 3.6) shows the history of Kroger Co.'s stock price since 1980. Based on this graph, you reckon that the stock price will remain above $14 within the next three years.

  i. Compute the probability that $S_T > 14$ using the implied distribution.

  ii. Compute the value of the "capped quadratic" option conditional upon $\{S_T > 14\}$. Is this an arbitrage price?

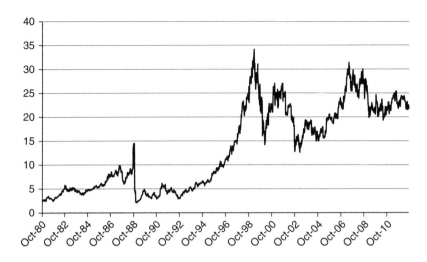

FIGURE 3.6   Historical price of Kroger Co.'s stock since 1980.

3.5   Path-Dependent Payoff

Consider an option whose payoff at maturity T_2 is a nonlinear function $f(S_{T_1}, S_{T_2})$ of the future underlying spot price observed at times $T_1 < T_2$.

(a) Give two classical examples of such an option.
(b) Write the pseudo-code to price this option in the Black-Scholes model using the Monte Carlo method.
(c) Assume that the implied distributions of both S_{T_1} and S_{T_2} are known. Can you think of a method to find "the" value of the option? If yes provide the pseudo-code; if not explain what information you are missing.

3.6   Delta

Modify the code from Section 3-3 to calculate the delta of the "capped quadratic" option. *Hint: Write $\sigma^*(S_0, K) \equiv \sigma^*(K/S_0)$ and carefully amend Equation (3.2) accordingly.*

CHAPTER 4

Local Volatility and Beyond

The local volatility model was independently developed in the early 1990s by Derman and Kani and by Dupire. It has arguably become the benchmark model to price and hedge a wide range of equity exotics such as digitals, Asians, and barriers, but fails on certain payoffs such as forward start options, which are better approached using a stochastic volatility model. The model can be difficult to implement since it requires a high-quality, smooth implied volatility surface as input, and simulation of all intermediate spot prices until maturity using short time steps.

4-1   LOCAL VOLATILITY TREES

The local volatility model is best visualized on a binomial tree: instead of using the same volatility parameter to generate the tree of future spot prices (Figure 4.1) the local volatility model uses a different volatility parameter at every node (Figure 4.2). The option is then priced as usual using backward induction.

Given a local volatility function $\sigma_{\mathrm{loc}}(t,S)$ it is relatively easy to construct a tree and then compute the corresponding model-implied volatilities $\sigma^*(K, T)$. A step-by-step guide can be found in Derman and Kani (1994).

In practice we are faced with the reverse problem: given market-implied volatilities $\sigma^*(K, T)$ for a finite set of strikes and maturities, we want to find the corresponding local volatilities $\sigma_{\mathrm{loc}}(t, S)$. This leads to an unstable calibration problem where a small change in input may produce very different results.

We will not venture into these topics, mostly because finite difference and Monte Carlo methods are now preferred to tree methods.

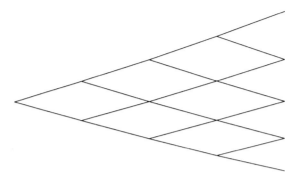

FIGURE 4.1 Binomial tree with constant volatility.

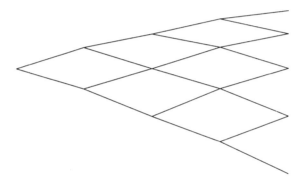

FIGURE 4.2 Binomial tree with local volatility.

4-2 LOCAL VOLATILITY IN CONTINUOUS TIME

The continuous time formulation of the local volatility model is that the spot price process is a diffusion of the form:

$$dS_t/S_t = \mu_t dt + \sigma_{\text{loc}}(t, S_t)dW_t$$

where the drift μ_t is irrelevant because it will disappear under the risk-neutral measure, and $\sigma_{\text{loc}}(t, S)$ is a function which is uniquely determined when the entire implied volatility surface $\sigma^*(K, T)$ is known.

In practice it is best to start with a smooth implied volatility surface such as an SVI fit to option market data and compute local volatilities by means of Dupire's equation (see Section 4-3.1).

With the local volatility function in hand, time-dependent exotic pay-offs may be priced using Monte Carlo simulations. The Euler-Maruyama discretization method provides an easy way to simulate a single path along discrete time steps of length Δt by iterating the formula:

$$S_{t+\Delta t} = S_t \left[1 + v_t \Delta t + \sigma_{\text{loc}} \left(t, S_t \right) \tilde{\varepsilon}_t \sqrt{\Delta t} \right]$$

where v_t is the risk-neutral drift (forward interest rate minus dividend rate) at time t and $\tilde{\varepsilon}_t$ is a standard normal.

Figure 4.3 compares a simulated path using the local volatility model with its corresponding geometric Brownian motion. We can see that the two paths differ somewhat significantly.

It is worth noting that the Euler-Maruyama method might occasionally produce negative prices, particularly when Δt is too large. This will happen whenever $\tilde{\varepsilon}_t < \frac{-1-v_t \Delta t}{\sigma_{\text{loc}}(t,S_t)\sqrt{\Delta t}}$.

More efficient discretization methods such as Milstein's are also available in order to improve the accuracy of simulated paths, at the cost of additional computations.

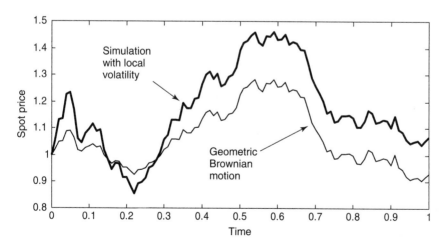

FIGURE 4.3 Simulated path with local volatility and corresponding geometric Brownian motion.

4-3 CALCULATING LOCAL VOLATILITIES

4-3.1 Dupire's Equation

When all call prices $c(K, T)$ are available for a continuum of strikes $K > 0$ and maturities $T > 0$—such as call prices generated by an implied volatility surface model—the local volatilities are given by Dupire's equation:

$$\sigma_{\text{loc}}^2(T, K) = \frac{\dfrac{\partial c}{\partial T}}{\dfrac{1}{2}K^2 \dfrac{\partial^2 c}{\partial K^2}} \tag{4.1}$$

provided interest and dividend rates are zero and c is $C^{2,1}$ (twice continuously differentiable with respect to K and continuously differentiable with respect to T). In other words, local volatility at time T and level K is proportional to the price ratio of an instant calendar spread to an infinitesimal butterfly spread.

We can get the intuition behind Equation (4.1) by rewriting $c(K, T) = c(t, S_t, K, T)$ and making the approximation that, conditional upon $S_T = K$, the local volatility $\sigma_{\text{loc}}(T, K)$ is constant over the interval $[T, T + \Delta T]$. Then:

- Using the rule of thumb that for constant volatility σ an at-the-money call is approximately worth[1] $c(t, K, K, T) \approx \frac{1}{\sqrt{2\pi}} K\sigma\sqrt{T - t}$, we get $\frac{\partial c}{\partial T}(t, K, K, T) \approx \frac{K}{2\sqrt{2\pi(T-t)}}\sigma$ and thus $\frac{\partial c}{\partial T}(T, K, K, T + \Delta T) \approx \frac{K}{2\sqrt{2\pi\Delta T}}\sigma_{\text{loc}}(T, K)$.

- Ignoring time value of money, the denominator is proportional to the implied distribution $\frac{\partial^2 c}{\partial K^2}$, which reduces to the Black-Scholes lognormal distribution $\frac{N'(d_2)}{K\sigma\sqrt{T-t}}$ when volatility is constant. Thus $\frac{1}{2}K^2 \frac{\partial^2 c}{\partial K^2}(T, K, K, T + \Delta T) \approx \frac{1}{2}K^2 \frac{N'(d_2)}{K\sigma_{\text{loc}}(T,K)\sqrt{\Delta T}} \approx \frac{K}{2\sqrt{2\pi\Delta T}} \frac{1}{\sigma_{\text{loc}}(T,K)}$ since $N'(d_2) \approx \frac{1}{\sqrt{2\pi}}$ at the money.

Taking the ratio of the two quantities and simplifying, we get $\sigma_{\text{loc}}^2(T, K)$ as required. A more rigorous derivation of Equation (4.1) is given in Appendix 4.A.

In practice, local volatilities can be difficult to compute, particularly for deeply out-of-the-money strikes and when input call prices are directly taken from the market without careful interpolation techniques. In particular,

---

[1]See, for example, Bossu and Henrotte (2012), Chapter 7, Problem 8.

approximating $\frac{\partial^2 c}{\partial K^2}$ with finite differences can create instability because this quantity is very small for deeply out-of-the-money strikes.

There are two standard approaches to address this issue:

1. Specify local volatility in functional parametric form and calibrate to option prices
2. Specify the implied volatility surface in functional parametric form and compute the corresponding local volatility surface

We now describe the second approach.

4-3.2 From Implied Volatility to Local Volatility

Assuming that the implied volatility surface $\sigma^*(K, T)$ is known and smooth, we can directly compute the corresponding local volatility surface by substituting into Equation (4.1) the derivatives of $c(K, T) = c_{BS}(S, K, T, \sigma^*(K, T))$ (see Problem 4.1). After calculations we obtain:

$$\sigma_{\text{loc}}^2(T, K) = \sigma^{*2}$$

$$\times \frac{1 + \dfrac{2T}{\sigma^*}\dfrac{\partial \sigma^*}{\partial T}}{1 + 2d_1\left(K\dfrac{\partial \sigma^*}{\partial K}\sqrt{T}\right) + d_1 d_2\left(K\dfrac{\partial \sigma^*}{\partial K}\sqrt{T}\right)^2 + \left(K\dfrac{\partial^2 \sigma^*}{\partial K^2}\sqrt{T}\right)\left(K\sigma^*\sqrt{T}\right)}$$

$$(4.2)$$

where for ease of notation we omitted evaluations at (K, T) for σ^* and its partial derivatives. Note that rates and dividends are again assumed to be zero.

As unpalatable as it may look, this formula tends to be relatively stable numerically, provided the implied volatility surface supplied as input is smooth. Figure 4.4 compares the implied and local volatility surfaces obtained from Gurrieri's (2010) model fitted to S&P 500 option prices. We can see that for fixed maturity the slope or skew of the local volatility curve is steeper.

4-3.3 Hedging with Local Volatility

The local volatility model produces the same delta as the implied volatility surface, which is higher than the Black-Scholes delta using a sticky-moneyness or sticky-delta rule. This consistency is another attractive feature of the local volatility model.

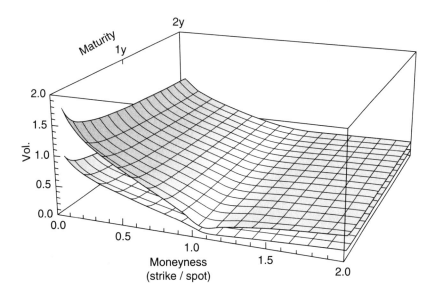

FIGURE 4.4 Local volatility surface (top) vs. implied volatility surface (bottom), fitted to S&P 500 option prices as of August 29, 2012. Implied volatilities were shifted down by 0.1 to better separate the two surfaces.

4-4 STOCHASTIC VOLATILITY

As stated in the introduction, the local volatility model can be used to price a wide range of equity exotics, but not all. In particular, forward start and cliquet options depend heavily on the future evolution of the implied volatility surface and require a more sophisticated approach.

There are many ways to define stochastic volatility, but most models tend to specify joint spot price and instant volatility dynamics, that is:

- A stochastic differential equation for the underlying spot price process, or sometimes the forward price process, which is typically of the form:

$$dS_t/S_t = \mu(\cdots)dt + \sqrt{v_t}dW_t \qquad (4.3)$$

  where W is a standard Brownian motion, μ can be anything, and v_t denotes instant variance;

- A stochastic differential equation for instant variance, typically of the form:

$$dv_t = \alpha_t dt + \omega_t dZ_t \qquad (4.4)$$

  where Z is a standard Brownian motion with correlation $(dW_t)(dZ_t) \equiv \rho_t dt$, α_t is the instant variance drift, and ω_t is the volatility of instant variance. Note that in general α, ω, ρ could be stochastic processes driven by other sources of randomness than W and Z.

The Heston and Carr-Wu LNV models (see Section 2-4.2.3) are examples of such models under risk-neutral probabilities.

To a degree, the local volatility model may be seen as an elementary stochastic volatility model in which instant variance $v_t = \sigma_{loc}^2(t, S_t)$ has perfect correlation of ± 1 with the stock price. When correlation is not perfect, a connection persists in the form of conditional expectations (see Section 4-4.2). As such the local volatility function may be seen as the backbone of every stochastic volatility model of the form (4.3) and (4.4).

Note that some authors focus on (4.3) without specifying (4.4) (e.g., Carr and Wu (2011)) while others ditch (4.3) and only focus on (4.4) (e.g., Bossu (2005)).

Because instant variance is not a tradable asset (nor even an observable quantity), its drift may be of significance, and modelers often stipulate mean reversion in its definition. This is the case of the Heston model, whose drift $\kappa(\bar{v} - v_t)$ will be more strongly positive or negative as v_t goes further away from the long-run variance $\bar{v}$, pulling v_t back towards $\bar{v}$.

Note, however, that with the development of variance swap markets (see Section 5-2), total variance $V_T = \int_0^T v_t dt \equiv \int_0^T \left(\ln \frac{S_{t+dt}}{S_t} \right)^2 dt$ has become tradable. We may thus compare $\mathbb{E}(V_T) = \int_0^T \mathbb{E}(v_t) dt$ to market prices to calibrate the model and assess its quality.

4-4.1 Hedging Theory

When the instant variance process is an Ito process, one major theoretical adjustment caused by stochastic volatility models of the form (4.3) and (4.4) is the addition of an ancillary option as hedging instrument.

We now provide a slightly modified version of the hedging argument followed by Wilmott (2006). Assuming that all option values $f(t, S_t, v_t)$ depend only on time, spot, and instant volatility, we have by the multidimensional Ito-Doeblin theorem:

$$df_t = \frac{\partial f}{\partial t} dt + \frac{\partial f}{\partial S} dS_t + \frac{\partial f}{\partial v} dv_t + \frac{1}{2} \left[\frac{\partial^2 f}{\partial S^2} (dS_t)^2 + 2 \frac{\partial^2 f}{\partial S \partial v} (dS_t)(dv_t) + \frac{\partial^2 f}{\partial v^2} (dv_t)^2 \right],$$

that is:

$$df_t = \left[\frac{\partial f}{\partial t} + \frac{1}{2} \frac{\partial^2 f}{\partial S^2} v_t S_t^2 + \frac{1}{2} \frac{\partial^2 f}{\partial v^2} \omega_t^2 + \frac{\partial^2 f}{\partial S \partial v} \rho_t \omega_t \sqrt{v_t} S_t \right] dt + \frac{\partial f}{\partial S} dS_t + \frac{\partial f}{\partial v} dv_t.$$

Because df_t is exposed to two sources of risk, namely dS_t contingent on W and dv_t contingent on Z, which is correlated with W, perfect hedging requires trading S and another option g on the same underlying asset S with value $g(t, S_t, v_t)$. Specifically, we must sell a quantity $\delta_g = \frac{\partial f}{\partial v} \Big/ \frac{\partial g}{\partial v}$ of g to cancel

dv_t terms; the variation in value Π of the corresponding portfolio long one option f and short δ_g options g is then:

$$d\Pi_t = [\gamma_{f,t} - \delta_g \gamma_{g,t}]dt + \left(\frac{\partial f}{\partial S} - \delta_g \frac{\partial g}{\partial S} \right) dS_t$$

where $\gamma_{f,t} = \frac{\partial f}{\partial t} + \frac{1}{2}\frac{\partial^2 f}{\partial S^2}v_t S_t^2 + \frac{1}{2}\frac{\partial^2 f}{\partial v^2}\omega_t^2 + \frac{\partial^2 f}{\partial S \partial v}\rho_t \omega_t \sqrt{v_t}S_t$ is the drift coefficient for option f and $\gamma_{g,t}$ is defined similarly with respect to option g.

We may now sell a quantity $\delta_S = \frac{\partial f}{\partial S} - \delta_g \frac{\partial g}{\partial S}$ of S to obtain a riskless portfolio long one option f, short δ_g options g and short δ_S units of S, whose value P must grow at the risk-free rate under penalty of arbitrage. Thus,

$$r(f_t - \delta_g g_t - \delta_S S_t) = \gamma_{f,t} - \delta_g \gamma_{g,t}$$

Substituting $\delta_S = \frac{\partial f}{\partial S} - \delta_g \frac{\partial g}{\partial S}, \delta_g = \frac{\partial f}{\partial v} / \frac{\partial g}{\partial v}$ and rearranging terms we obtain the remarkable identity:

$$\frac{rf_t - rS_t \frac{\partial f}{\partial S} - \gamma_{f,t}}{\frac{\partial f}{\partial v}} = \frac{rg_t - rS_t \frac{\partial g}{\partial S} - \gamma_{g,t}}{\frac{\partial g}{\partial v}}$$

Because the left-hand side only depends on f while the right-hand side only depends on g, and because f and g can be chosen arbitrarily, we conclude that all option values must satisfy the pricing equation:

$$rf_t - rS_t \frac{\partial f}{\partial S} - \gamma_{f,t} = \Lambda_t \frac{\partial f}{\partial v}$$

for some "universal" function $\Lambda_t = \Lambda(t, S_t, v_t)$ common to all options.

It turns out that Λ_t is the risk-neutral drift of instant variance. Indeed, under risk-neutral probabilities we must have $\mathbb{E}_t(dS_t) = rS_t dt$ and $\mathbb{E}_t(df_t) = rf_t dt$. Taking conditional expectations of:

$$df_t = \gamma_{f,t}dt + \frac{\partial f}{\partial S}dS_t + \frac{\partial f}{\partial v}dv_t$$

and making these substitutions we get $rf_t dt = \gamma_{f,t}dt + \frac{\partial f}{\partial S}rS_t dt + \frac{\partial f}{\partial v}\mathbb{E}_t(dv_t)$, leaving $\mathbb{E}_t(dv_t) = \Lambda_t dt$ after all cancellations.

In theory Λ_t could be implied from option prices, but this is very difficult to achieve in practice. Instead, most models specify the risk-neutral dynamics of instant variance directly, which amounts to specifying Λ_t. In the case of the Heston model we have:

$$\Lambda_t = \Lambda(t, S_t, v_t) = \kappa(\bar{v} - v_t)$$

which is algebraically independent from the spot price S_t. Note, however, that S_t and v_t are *not* statistically independent if $\rho_t \not\equiv 0$.

4-4.2   Connection with Local Volatility

It can be shown (see, e.g., Gatheral (2005), who follows Derman and Kani (1997)) that within the framework (4.3) and (4.4) the conditional expectation of stochastic instant variance v_t upon the spot price S_t must be the local variance:

$$\mathbb{E}(v_t | S_t = S) = \sigma_{\text{loc}}^2(t, S)$$

This is a remarkable property, which further underscores the significance of the local volatility concept.

It should be emphasized that stochastic volatility models such as Heston typically violate this property when local volatilities are computed from option market prices. This will happen with all models that do not exactly match the market's implied volatility surface.

As an interesting corollary, by iterated expectations the undiscounted price of total variance reduces to the expected total local variance:

$$\mathbb{E}\left(\int_0^T v_t dt \right) = \mathbb{E}\left[\int_0^T \sigma_{\text{loc}}^2\left(t, S_t\right) dt \right]$$

which explains why the local volatility model correctly prices variance swaps (see Section 5-2) even though it does not provide a correct replication strategy. Note how the expectation on the right-hand side need not involve v at all.

4-4.3   Monte Carlo Method

An attractive feature of stochastic volatility models is that, once they have been satisfactorily calibrated to vanilla options prices, it is relatively easy to price exotics by Monte Carlo simulations. This may be done by Euler-Maruyama discretization of Equations (4.3) and (4.4) with short time steps of length Δt:

$$\begin{cases} v_{t+\Delta t} = v_t + \Lambda_t \Delta t + \omega_t \left(\rho_t \tilde{\varepsilon}_{1,t} + \sqrt{1 - \rho_t^2} \tilde{\varepsilon}_{2,t} \right) \sqrt{\Delta t} \\ S_{t+\Delta t} = S_t \left[1 + (r - q)\, \Delta t + \sqrt{v_t} \tilde{\varepsilon}_{1,t} \sqrt{\Delta t} \right] \end{cases}$$

where Λ_t is the risk-neutral drift of v_t, r and q are respectively the continuous interest and dividend rates, and $\tilde{\varepsilon}_{1,t}$, $\tilde{\varepsilon}_{2,t}$ are independent standard normals.

In practice the Euler-Maruyama scheme may produce negative instant variance when Δt is too large or Feller conditions are disregarded.

A quick-and-dirty fix is then to reset v_t at zero, but for some models this might mean that v_t gets stuck there, so this fix should be used with caution. Another common fix is to take absolute values.

More sophisticated simulation methods targeting the Heston model have been put forward in recent years. A good reference is Andersen (2007), which reviews several schemes and develops new ones.

4-4.4 Pricing and Hedging Forward Start Options

Recall that a forward start call option with maturity T has its strike set at a future date $0 < t_0 < T$, usually as a percentage k of the future spot price S_{t_0}. For example consider a one-year at-the-money call starting one month forward. After a month, this option will become a regular one-year[2] vanilla call with strike $K = S_{1/12}$, at which point it will be approximately worth $\frac{S_{1/12}}{\sqrt{2\pi}}\sigma^*(S_{1/12}, 1)$ if interest and dividend rates are close to zero.

To price the forward start call we thus need to compute $\frac{1}{\sqrt{2\pi}}e^{-r/12}\mathbb{E}[S_{1/12}\ \sigma^*(S_{1/12}, 1)]$, whence the relevance of stochastic volatility models. Note that the use of the risk-free interest rate r, rather than a higher rate adjusted for risk, is justified by the theoretical existence of a riskless hedging portfolio.

In practice it turns out that the price of an at-the-money forward start option is not significantly different using a stochastic volatility model such as Heston or using the local volatility model. This is because the price is approximately linear in volatility. For out-of-the-money forward start options, however, the difference is more significant because there is some convexity in volatility known as volga.

In terms of hedging, it should be emphasized that stochastic volatility models rely on both continuous delta- and vega-hedging using the underlying asset and another option. This is very impractical because of higher transaction costs that are incurred on option markets and exotic traders tend to only execute the initial vega-hedge and charge extra for residual volga risk.

4-4.5 A Word on Stochastic Volatility Models with Jumps

A popular theoretical extension for stochastic volatility models is the addition of jumps; that is, sudden spot price discontinuities. We do not discuss

---

[2]Note that in this example the actual maturity of the forward start option is 13 months at inception. In some cases the nominal maturity might mean the actual maturity, from which the forward start period should be subtracted, so one must always double-check to see which convention applies.

these models, mostly because jumps of random size cannot be hedged and the riskless dynamic arbitrage argument thus breaks down. Two accessible references here are Gatheral (2005) and Wilmott (2006).

REFERENCES

Andersen, Leif B. G. 2007. "Efficient Simulation of the Heston Stochastic Volatility Model." Working paper. Available at http://ssrn.com/abstract=946405 or http://dx.doi.org/10.2139/ssrn.946405.

Bossu, Sébastien. 2005. "Arbitrage pricing of equity correlation swaps." JPMorgan Equity Derivatives Report.

Bossu, Sébastien, and Philippe Henrotte. 2012. *An Introduction to Equity Derivatives: Theory and Practice*, 2nd ed. Chichester, UK: John Wiley & Sons.

Carr, Peter and Liuren Wu. 2011. "A New Simple Approach for Constructing Implied Volatility Surfaces." Working paper.

Derman, Emanuel, and Iraj Kani. 1994. "The Volatility Smile and Its Implied Tree." Goldman Sachs Quantitative Strategies Research Notes, January.

Derman, Emanuel, and Iraj Kani. 1997. "Stochastic Implied Trees: Arbitrage Pricing With Stochastic Term and Strike Structure of Volatility." Goldman Sachs Quantitative Strategies Research Notes, April.

Dupire, Bruno. 1994. "Pricing with a Smile." *Risk* 7 (1): 18–20.

Gatheral, Jim. 2005. *The Volatility Surface*. Hoboken, NJ: John Wiley & Sons.

Gurrieri, Sébastien. 2010. "A Class of Term Structures for SVI Implied Volatility", Working paper. Available at http://ssrn.com/abstract=1779463 or http://dx.doi.org/10.2139/ssrn.1779463.

Wilmott, Paul. 2006. *Paul Wilmott on Quantitative Finance*, 2nd ed. Hoboken, NJ: John Wiley & Sons.

PROBLEMS

4.1   From Implied to Local Volatility

(a) Assume zero rates and dividends. Given $\frac{\partial c_{BS}}{\partial T} = \frac{KN'(d_2)\sigma}{2\sqrt{T}}$ and $\frac{\partial c_{BS}}{\partial \sigma} = K\sqrt{T}N'(d_2)$ establish Equation (4.2). *Hint: Consult Problem 2.2.*

(b) Show that if there is no implied volatility smile—that is, σ^* is only a function of maturity—then: $\frac{1}{T}\int_0^T \sigma_{loc}^2(t, S_t)dt = \sigma^{*2}(T)$. *Hint: Calculate* $\frac{d}{dT}(T\sigma^{*2}(T))$.

(c) Show that if σ^* is only a linear function of strike close to at-the-money, then $\sigma_{\text{loc}}(T, K) \approx \frac{\sigma^*(K)}{1 + d_1 K \sigma^{*\prime}(K)\sqrt{T}}$ and thus $\frac{\partial \sigma_{\text{loc}}}{\partial K} \approx 2\sigma^{*\prime}(K)$. *Hint: Show that*

$$\sigma_{\text{loc}}^2(T, K) = \frac{\sigma^{*2}(K)}{(1 + d_1 K \sigma^{*\prime}(K)\sqrt{T})^2 - \sigma^* d_1 \sqrt{T}(K\sigma^{*\prime}(K)\sqrt{T})^2} \text{ and then assume that the}$$

term in $(\sigma^{*\prime}(K))^2$ *is negligible.*

4.2 Market Price of Volatility Risk

Consider the stochastic volatility framework of (4.3) and (4.4) and define $\lambda_t = \frac{\alpha_t - \Lambda_t}{\omega_t}$. Let $f_t = f(t, S_t, v_t)$ be the value of an option on the underlying asset S.

(a) Suppose we only delta-hedge the option. Using the Ito-Doeblin theorem show that the change in value of the hedging portfolio is $d\Pi_t = \gamma_{f,t}dt + \frac{\partial f}{\partial v}dv_t$

(b) Show that $d\Pi_t - r\Pi_t dt = \lambda_t \omega_t \frac{\partial f}{\partial v}dt + \omega_t \frac{\partial f}{\partial v}dZ_t$

(c) Examine the conditional expectation and standard deviation at time t of $\frac{d\Pi_t}{\Pi_t}$ and explain why λ_t is called the "market price of volatility risk."

4.3 Local Volatility Pricing

Consider an underlying stock S currently trading at $S_0 = 100$ that does not pay any dividend. Assume the implied volatility function is $\sigma_{\text{loc}}(t, S) = 0.1 + \frac{0.1 - 0.15 \times \ln(S/S_0)}{\sqrt{t}}$, and that interest rates are zero.

(a) Produce the graph of the corresponding local volatility surface using Equation (4.2) for spots 0 to 200 and maturities zero to five years.

(b) Write a Monte Carlo algorithm to price the following one-year payoffs using 252 time steps and, for example, 10,000 paths:

- "Capped quadratic" option: $\min\left(1, \frac{S_1^2}{S_0^2}\right)$
- Asian at-the-money-call: $\max\left(0, \frac{S_{0.25} + S_{0.5} + S_{0.75} + S_1}{4 \times S_0} - 1\right)$
- Barrier call: $\max(0, S_1 - S_0)$ if S always traded above 80 using 252 daily observations, 0 otherwise.

APPENDIX 4.A: DERIVATION OF DUPIRE'S EQUATION

For diffusion processes of the form:

$$dX_t = a(t, X_t)dt + b(t, X_t)dW_t$$

the probability density $\pi(t, x) = \mathbb{P}\{X_t = x\}$ must solve the forward Kolmogorov equation:

$$\frac{\partial \pi}{\partial t} = -\frac{\partial}{\partial x}(a\pi) + \frac{1}{2}\frac{\partial^2}{\partial x^2}(b^2\pi)$$

When interest rates are zero, the risk-neutral spot price process with local volatility is simply:

$$dS_t = \sigma_{\text{loc}}(t, S_t)S_t dW_t$$

and the forward Kolmogorov equation at time T reduces to:

$$\frac{\partial \pi}{\partial T}(T, S) = \frac{1}{2}\frac{\partial^2}{\partial S^2}(S^2\sigma_{\text{loc}}^2(T, S)\pi(T, S))$$

Additionally, the price of the call struck at K with maturity T is $c(K, T) = \int_K^\infty (S - K)\pi(T, S)dS$. Taking the derivative with respect to T and substituting the forward Kolmogorov equation we get:

$$\frac{dc}{dT} = \int_K^\infty (S - K)\frac{\partial \pi}{\partial T}(T, S)dS = \frac{1}{2}\int_K^\infty (S - K)\frac{\partial^2}{\partial S^2}(S^2\sigma_{\text{loc}}^2(T, S)\pi(T, S))dS$$

Integrating by parts we get:

$$\frac{dc}{dT} = \frac{1}{2}\left[(S - K)\frac{\partial}{\partial S}(S^2\sigma_{\text{loc}}^2(T, S)\pi(T, S))\right]_K^\infty - \frac{1}{2}\int_K^\infty \frac{\partial}{\partial S}(S^2\sigma_{\text{loc}}^2(T, S)\pi(T, S))dS$$

$$= \frac{1}{2}K^2\sigma_{\text{loc}}^2(T, K)\pi(T, K)$$

which is Dupire's equation after recognizing the implied distribution density $\pi = \frac{\partial^2 c}{\partial K^2}$. Note that we assumed all quantities taken as $S \to \infty$ to vanish, which is verified in all practical applications.

CHAPTER 5

Volatility Derivatives

Option traders who hedge their delta have long realized that their option book is exposed to many other market variables, chief of which is volatility. In fact we will see that the P&L on a delta-hedged option position is driven by the spread between two types of volatility: the instant realized volatility of the underlying stock or stock index, and the option's implied volatility. Thus option traders are specialists of volatility, and naturally they want to trade it directly. This prompted the creation of a new generation of derivatives: forward contracts and options on volatility itself.

5-1 VOLATILITY TRADING

Delta-hedged options may be used to trade volatility, specifically the gap between implied volatility σ^* and realized volatility σ—another word for historical volatility. To see this consider the P&L breakdown of an option position over a time interval Δt:

$$\text{P\&L}_{\Delta t} = \delta \times (\Delta S) + \frac{1}{2}\Gamma \times (\Delta S)^2 + \Theta \times (\Delta t) + \rho \times (\Delta r) + \mathcal{V} \times (\Delta \sigma^*) + \cdots$$

where δ, Γ, Θ, ρ, $\mathcal{V}$ are the option's Greeks, ΔS is the change in underlying spot price, Δr is the change in interest rate, $\Delta \sigma^*$ is the change in implied volatility, and "$\cdots$" are high-order terms completing the Taylor expansion.

Assuming that the option is delta-hedged, the interest rate and implied volatility are constant, and high-order terms are negligible, we may write:

$$\text{P\&L}_{\Delta t} \approx \frac{1}{2}\Gamma \times (\Delta S)^2 + \Theta \times (\Delta t)$$

From the Black-Scholes partial differential equation we get $\Theta \approx -\frac{1}{2}\Gamma S^2 \sigma^{*2}$ where S is the initial spot price. Substituting this result and factoring by the dollar gamma $\frac{1}{2}\Gamma S^2$ we obtain the P&L proxy equation:

$$\text{P\&L}_{\Delta t} \approx \frac{1}{2}\Gamma S^2 \left[\left(\frac{\Delta S}{S} \right)^2 - \left(\sigma^* \sqrt{\Delta t} \right)^2 \right]$$

The quantity $\left(\frac{\Delta S}{S} \right)^2$ is the squared realized return on the underlying asset; for short Δt it may be viewed as instant realized variance. The delta-hedged option's P&L is thus determined by the difference between realized and implied variances multiplied by the dollar gamma. In particular, for positive dollar gamma, the P&L is positive whenever realized variance exceeds implied variance, breaks even when both quantities are equal, and is negative whenever realized variance is lower than implied variance.

If the option is delta-hedged at N regular intervals of length Δt until maturity, the cumulative P&L proxy equation is then:

$$\text{Cumulative P\&L} \approx \frac{1}{2} \sum_{t=0}^{N-1} \Gamma_t S_t^2 \left[\left(\frac{\Delta S_t}{S_t} \right)^2 - \left(\sigma^* \sqrt{\Delta t} \right)^2 \right] \qquad (5.1)$$

which captures the difference between realized and implied variances weighted by dollar gammas over the option's lifetime.

The continuous-time version of Equation (5.1) was derived by Carr and Madan (1998) and is exact rather than approximate:

$$\text{Cumulative P\&L} = \frac{1}{2} \int_0^T e^{r(T-t)} \Gamma_t S_t^2 \left[\sigma_t^2 - \sigma^{*2} \right] dt \qquad (5.2)$$

where r is the continuous interest rate and σ_t is the instant realized volatility at time t.

In practice this rather clear picture is blurred by the fact that implied volatility varies over time, impacting hedge ratios and thus P&L.

The cumulative P&L equations also have another interpretation: An option issuer is in the business of underwriting option payoffs and then replicating them by trading the underlying asset. In the Black-Scholes world, such replication is riskless, but in practice there is a mismatch given by the cumulative P&L equations (subject to their assumptions). At times the mismatch is negative, and at other times it is positive, resulting in a distribution of possible P&L outcomes. By the law of large numbers and the central-limit theorem, repeating option transactions often for a small profit narrows the P&L distribution of the option book and results in positive revenues on average.

5-2   VARIANCE SWAPS

Variance swaps appeared in the mid-1990s as a means to trade (the square of) volatility directly rather than through delta-hedging. Their attractive property is that they can be approximately replicated with a static portfolio of vanilla options, providing a robust fair price.

Recently the Chicago Board Options Exchange (CBOE) launched a redesigned version of their variance futures with a quotation system matching over-the-counter (OTC) conventions. This interesting initiative may signal a shift from OTC to listed markets for variance swaps.

5-2.1   Variance Swap Payoff

From the buyer's viewpoint, the payoff of a variance swap on an underlying S with strike K_{var} and maturity T is:

$$\text{Variance Swap Payoff} = 10,000 \times (\sigma^2_{Realized} - K^2_{var})$$

where $\sigma_{Realized}$ is the annualized realized volatility of the N daily log-returns on S between $t = 0$ and $t = T$ under zero-mean assumption:

$$\sigma_{Realized} = \sqrt{\frac{252}{N} \sum_{i=0}^{N-1} \ln^2 \frac{S_{i+1}}{S_i}}$$

For example, a one-year variance swap on the S&P 500 struck at 25% pays off $10,000 \times (0.26^2 - 0.25^2) = \$51$ if realized volatility ends up at 26%. Figure 5.1 shows the variance swap payoff as a function of realized volatility. We can see that the shape is convex quadratic, which implies that

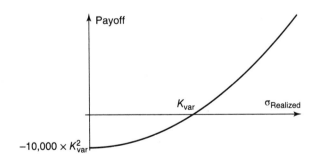

FIGURE 5.1   Variance swap payoff as a function of realized volatility.

profits are amplified and losses are discounted as realized volatility goes away from the strike.

In practice the quantity of variance swaps is often specified in "vega notional," for example, $100,000. This means that, close to the strike, each realized volatility point in excess of the strike pays off approximately $100,000. This is achieved by setting the actual quantity, called variance notional or variance units as:

$$\text{Variance units} = \frac{\text{Vega notional}}{200 \times K_{\text{var}}}$$

For example, with a 25% strike and $100,000 vega notional, the number of variance units is simply 2,000. If realized volatility is 26% the payoff is $2,000 \times [\$10,000 \times (.26^2 - .25^2)] = \$102,000$ which is close to the vega notional as required.

FOCUS ON VARIANCE FUTURES

The new variance futures launched by CBOE in December 2012 allow investors to trade variance swaps in a standardized format with all the benefits of listed securities: price transparency, market-making requirements, liquidity.

The futures are available in 1-, 2-, 3-, 6-, 9-, and 12-month rolling maturities. The strike is set the day before the start date (typically the third Friday of the month) using a VIX-type calculation (see Section 5-4).

Trading conventions were adjusted to reflect OTC market practices, in particular:

- Prices are quoted in terms of implied volatility, which may be compared against the fair value of future variance observed until maturity.

- The quantity is set to $1,000 vega notional, which is converted into variance units at trade execution.

- On the expiration date, the exchange will credit or debit the difference between realized variance and the square of strike, adjusted to cancel the effects of the daily variation margin.

5-2.2 Variance Swap Market

Variance swaps trade mostly over the counter. Table 5.1 shows mid-market prices for various underlyings and maturities.

TABLE 5.1 Variance Swap Mid-Market Prices on Three Stock Indexes as of August 21, 2013

Maturity	S&P 500	EuroStoxx 50	Nikkei 225
1 month	15.23	19.37	27.58
3 months	16.50	20.89	28.35
6 months	18.01	22.22	27.55
12 months	19.59	23.88	26.98
18 months	20.43	24.50	26.22
24 months	21.20	25.12	26.16

5-2.3 Variance Swap Hedging and Pricing

As stated earlier, variance swaps can be replicated using a static portfolio of calls and puts of the same maturity, which must then be delta-hedged. To see this, we must explicate the connection between variance swaps and the log-contract whose payoff is $-\ln S_T/F$ where F is the forward price.

Applying the Ito-Doeblin theorem to $\ln S_t$ yields:

$$\ln \frac{S_T}{S_0} = \int_0^T \frac{1}{S_t} dS_t - \frac{1}{2} \int_0^T \frac{1}{S_t^2} (dS_t)^2 = \int_0^T \frac{1}{S_t} dS_t - \frac{1}{2} \int_0^T \sigma_t^2 dt$$

where σ_t is the underlying asset's instant volatility, which may be stochastic. Rearranging terms, we can see that realized variance may be replicated by continuously maintaining a position of $2/S_t$ in the underlying stock and holding onto a certain quantity of log-contracts:

$$\int_0^T \sigma_t^2 dt = 2 \int_0^T \frac{1}{S_t} dS_t - 2 \ln \frac{S_T}{S_0}$$

Assuming that the risk-neutral dynamics of the underlying price are of the form $dS_t = v_t S_t dt + \sigma_t S_t dW_t$ where v_t is the risk-neutral drift, we have

$$\mathbb{E}\left(\int_0^T \frac{1}{S_t} dS_t \right) = \mathbb{E}\left(\int_0^T v_t dt \right) = \ln \frac{F}{S_0} \text{ and thus the fair value of variance}$$

matches the fair value of two log-contracts:

$$\mathbb{E}\left(\int_0^T \sigma_t^2 dt \right) = \mathbb{E}\left(-2 \ln \frac{S_T}{F} \right)$$

The log-contract does not trade, but from Section 3-2 we know that any European payoff can be decomposed as a portfolio of calls and puts struck along a continuum of strikes. Specifically we have the identity:

$$-\ln \frac{S_T}{F} = 1 - \frac{S_T}{F} + \int_0^F \frac{1}{K^2} \max(0, K - S_T) dK + \int_F^\infty \frac{1}{K^2} \max(0, S_T - K) dK$$

In other words the log-contract may be replicated with a portfolio which is:

- Short a forward contract on S struck at the forward price F
- Long all puts struck at $K < F$ in quantities dK / K^2
- Long all calls struck at $K > F$ in quantities dK / K^2

The corresponding fair value of annualized variance is then:

$$K_{var}^2 = \frac{2}{T}\mathbb{E}\left(-\ln\frac{S_T}{F}\right) = \frac{2e^{rT}}{T}\left[\int_0^F \frac{1}{K^2}p(K)\,dK + \int_F^\infty \frac{1}{K^2}c(K)dK\right]$$

where r is the interest rate for maturity T, $p(K)$ is the price of a put struck at K, and $c(K)$ is the price of a call struck at K.

In practice only a finite number of strikes are available, and we have the proxy formula:

$$K_{var}^2 \approx \frac{2e^{rT}}{T}\left[\sum_{i=1}^n \frac{p(K_i)}{K_i^2}\Delta K_i + \sum_{i=n+1}^{n+m} \frac{c(K_i)}{K_i^2}\Delta K_i\right], \qquad (5.3)$$

where $K_1 < \cdots < K_n \leq F \leq K_{n+1} < \cdots < K_{n+m}$ are the successive strikes of n puts worth $p(K_i)$ and m calls worth $c(K_i)$, and $\Delta K_i = K_i - K_{i-1}$ is the strike step.

A more accurate calculation based on overhedging of the log-contract is discussed in Demeterfi, Derman, Kamal, and Zhou (1999). An alternative derivation of the hedging portfolio and price based on the property that variance swaps have constant dollar gamma can be found in Bossu, Strasser, and Guichard (2005).

5-2.4 Forward Variance

Two variance swaps with maturities $T_1 < T_2$ may be combined to capture the **forward variance** observed between T_1 and T_2. Indeed under the zero-mean assumption variance is additive and thus:

$$T_1\sigma_{\text{Realized}}^2(0, T_1) + (T_2 - T_1)\sigma_{\text{Realized}}^2(T_1, T_2) = T_2\sigma_{\text{Realized}}^2(0, T_2)$$

where $\sigma_{\text{Realized}}^2(s, t)$ denotes realized volatility between times s and t. Thus:

$$\sigma_{\text{Realized}}^2(T_1, T_2) = \frac{T_2}{T_2 - T_1}\sigma_{\text{Realized}}^2(0, T_2) - \frac{T_1}{T_2 - T_1}\sigma_{\text{Realized}}^2(0, T_1)$$

This implies that the fair strike of a forward variance swap is:

$$K_{\text{var}}(T_1, T_2) = \sqrt{\frac{T_2}{T_2 - T_1} K_{\text{var}}^2(0, T_2) - \frac{T_1}{T_2 - T_1} K_{\text{var}}^2(0, T_1)}$$

and, when interest rates are zero, the corresponding hedge is long $\frac{T_2}{T_2 - T_1}$ variance swaps maturing at T_2 and short $\frac{T_1}{T_2 - T_1}$ variance swaps maturing at T_1.

When interest rates are non-zero, the quantity of the short leg should be adjusted to $\frac{T_1}{T_2 - T_1} e^{-r(T_2 - T_1)}$ because the near-term variance swap payoff at time T_1 will carry interest r between T_1 and T_2.

5-3 REALIZED VOLATILITY DERIVATIVES

Variance swaps are the simplest kind of realized volatility derivatives; that is, derivative contracts whose payoff is a function $f(\sigma_{\text{Realized}})$ of realized volatility. Other examples include:

- Volatility swaps, with payoff $\sigma_{\text{Realized}} - K_{\text{vol}}$
- Variance calls, with payoff $\max\left(0, \sigma_{\text{Realized}}^2 - K\right)$
- Variance puts, with payoff $\max\left(0, K - \sigma_{\text{Realized}}^2\right)$

Volatility swaps are offered by some banks to investors who prefer them to variance swaps. Deep out-of-the-money variance calls are often embedded in variance swap contracts on single stocks in the form of a cap on realized variance; this is because variance could "explode" when, for instance, the underlying stock is approaching bankruptcy.

Note that the volatility swap strike K_{vol} must be less than the variance swap strike K_{var} under penalty of arbitrage. This property may also be seen through Jensen's inequality:

$$K_{\text{vol}} = \mathbb{E}\left(\sqrt{\sigma_{\text{Realized}}^2}\right) \leq \sqrt{\mathbb{E}\left(\sigma_{\text{Realized}}^2\right)} = K_{\text{var}}$$

The ratio $\frac{K_{\text{var}}}{K_{\text{vol}}} \geq 1$ is called the convexity adjustment by practitioners.

Valuing realized volatility derivatives requires a model. Since realized variance is tradable, a natural idea here is to think of it as an underlying asset and apply standard option valuation theory.

However an adjustment is necessary to account for the fact that, as a tradable asset, realized variance is a mixture of past variance and future variance; specifically:

$$v_t = \frac{t}{T}\sigma^2(0,t) + \frac{T-t}{T}K_{var}^2(t,T) \qquad (5.4)$$

where v_t is the forward price of variance started at time 0 and ending at time T, $\sigma(0,t)$ is the historical volatility observed over $[0, t]$ and $K_{var}(t,T)$ is the fair strike at time t of a new variance swap expiring at time T.

Therefore we cannot assume that the volatility of v_t is constant as in the Black-Scholes model. Instead we may assume forward-neutral dynamics of the form:

$$dv_t/v_t = 2\omega\frac{T-t}{T}dW_t$$

where ω is a volatility of (future) volatility parameter and 2 is a conversion factor from volatility to variance.[1] In this fashion the diffusion coefficient $2\omega\frac{T-t}{T}$ linearly collapses to zero as we approach maturity, as suggested by Equation (5.4).

This simple modeling approach allows us to find closed-form formulas for the price of many realized volatility derivatives. For example, the fair strike of a volatility swap can be shown to be:

$$K_{vol} = K_{var}\exp\left(-\frac{1}{6}\omega^2 T\right)$$

and thus the convexity adjustment is simply $\frac{K_{var}}{K_{vol}} = \exp\left(\frac{1}{6}\omega^2 T\right)$.

Given K_{vol} and K_{var} from the market we may then estimate ω:

$$\omega = \sqrt{\frac{6}{T}\ln\frac{K_{var}}{K_{vol}}}$$

In practice volatility swaps are illiquid but, as suggested by Carr and Lee (2009), the fair value of realized volatility may be approximated with at-the-money implied volatility. For example, if one-year fair variance is 30% and one-year at-the-money implied volatility is 28%, we find $\omega \approx \sqrt{6\ln\frac{30\%}{28\%}} = 64.3\%$.

---

[1]Applying the Ito-Doeblin theorem to $\sqrt{v_t}$ we indeed obtain dynamics of the form $d\sqrt{v_t}/\sqrt{v_t} = \cdots dt + \omega\frac{T-t}{T}dW_t$.

5-4 IMPLIED VOLATILITY DERIVATIVES

Implied volatility derivatives are derivative contracts whose payoff is a function $f(\sigma_{\text{Implied}})$ of implied volatility. There are many choices for implied volatility and the most popular one is the Volatility Index (VIX) calculated by CBOE, which is the short-term fair variance derived from listed options on the S&P 500 in accordance with Equation (5.3).

The VIX is not a tradable asset, but CBOE nevertheless developed VIX futures and VIX options, which have become increasingly popular.

Specifically, the VIX is a *pro rata temporis* average of two subindexes based on front- and next-month[2] listed options in order to reflect the 30-day expected volatility. Each subindex is calculated according to the generalized formula:

$$\left(\frac{\text{VIX}}{100}\right)^2 = \frac{2e^{rT}}{T} \sum_i \frac{\Delta K_i}{K_i^2} Q(K_i) - \frac{1}{T}\left(\frac{F}{K_0} - 1\right)$$

where:

- T is the maturity
- r is the continuous interest rate for maturity T
- F is the forward price of the S&P 500 derived from listed option prices
- K_0 is the first strike below F
- K_i is the strike price of the *i*th out-of-the money listed option: a call if $i > 0$ and a put if $i < 0$
- ΔK_i is the interval between strike prices measured as $\frac{1}{2}(K_{i+1} - K_{i-1})$
- $Q(K_i)$ is the mid-price of the listed call or put struck at K_i.

There are many other practical details that can be found in the CBOE white paper on VIX (2009), such as how exactly the forward price is calculated or how the constituent options are selected.

5-4.1 VIX Futures

VIX futures are futures contracts on the VIX. On the settlement date T the following dollar amount is credited or debited by the exchange:

$$1{,}000 \times (\text{VIX}_T - \text{Fut}_t)$$

where 1,000 is the multiplication factor, VIX_T is the settlement level[3] of the VIX, and Fut_t is the trading price at time t.

---

[2]Or the second- and third-month listed options if front-month options expire in less than one week.

[3]Note that VIX futures do not settle the VIX itself but a special opening quotation of the VIX determined by automated auction of the constituent options prior to the opening of trading.

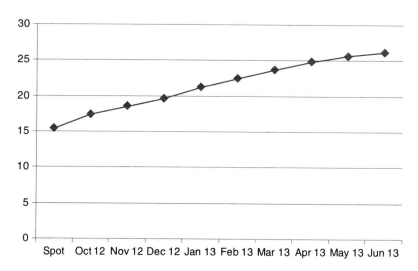

FIGURE 5.2 Term structure of VIX futures as of September 26, 2012.
Source: Bloomberg.

Figure 5.2 shows the term structure of VIX futures as of September 26, 2012. We can see that the curve is upward sloping; however, at times it may be downward sloping because VIX futures, contrary to stock or equity index futures, are not constrained by any carry arbitrage since the VIX is not a tradable asset.

It is worth emphasizing that VIX futures are bets on the future level of implied volatility, which itself is the market's guess at subsequent realized volatility. In this sense VIX futures are forward contracts on forward realized volatility—a potentially difficult level of "forwardness" to deal with.

Close to expiration, the futures tend to be highly correlated with the VIX. When futures expire in a month, they have about 0.5 correlation with the VIX. Futures that expire in five months or more exhibit almost no correlation.

5-4.2   VIX Options

VIX options are vanilla calls and puts on the VIX. On the settlement date T the following dollar amount is credited or debited by the exchange:

- For a call: $100 \times \max(0, \text{VIX}_T - K)$
- For a put: $100 \times \max(0, K - \text{VIX}_T)$

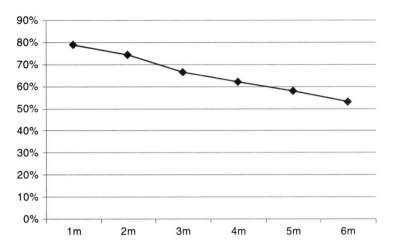

FIGURE 5.3 Implied volatility term structure of at-the-money VIX options as of September 26, 2012.
Source: Bloomberg.

where 100 is the multiplication factor, VIX_T is the settlement level[4] of the VIX, and K is the strike level.

For lack of a better consensus model, VIX option prices are commonly analyzed through Black's model to compute VIX implied volatilities. Figure 5.3 shows the term structure of at-the-money VIX implied volatility. We can see that the shape is downward sloping: short-term VIX futures are expected to be more volatile than long-term ones.

Similar to VIX futures, VIX option prices tend to have high correlation with the VIX close to expiration and low correlation far away from expiration.

Synthetic put-call parity holds for VIX options, which entails that VIX implied volatility is the same for calls and puts. Specifically:

VIX Call Price – VIX Put Price = Discount Factor

$$\times\ (\text{VIX Future Price} - \text{Strike})$$

where Discount Factor is the price of \$1 paid on the expiration date.

---

[4]Note that VIX options do not settle the VIX itself but a special opening quotation of the VIX determined by automated auction of the constituent options prior to the opening of trading.

REFERENCES

Bossu, Sébastien. 2005. "Arbitrage Pricing of Equity Correlation Swaps." JPMorgan Equity Derivatives report.

Bossu, Sébastien, Eva Strasser, and Régis Guichard. 2005. "Just What You Need to Know about Variance Swaps." JPMorgan Equity Derivatives report.

Carr, Peter, and Roger Lee. 2009. "Volatility Derivatives." *Annual Review of Financial Economics* 1: 1–21.

Carr, Peter, and Dilip Madan. 1998. "Towards a Theory of Volatility Trading." In *Volatility: New Estimation Techniques for Pricing Derivatives*, edited by R. Jarrow, 417–427. London: Risk Books.

"The CBOE Volatility Index—VIX." 2009. CBOE White Paper.

Demeterfi, Kresimir, Emanuel Derman, Michael Kamal, and Joseph Zhou. 1999. "More than You Ever Wanted to Know about Volatility Swaps." Goldman Sachs Quantitative Strategies Research Notes, March.

PROBLEMS

5.1   Delta-Hedging P&L Simulation

Consider a long position in 10,000 one-year at-the-money calls on ABC Inc.'s stock currently trading at \$100. Assume zero interest rates and dividends and 30% implied volatility.

(a) Suppose the "real" stock price process is a geometric Brownian motion with 5% drift and 29% realized volatility. Simulate the evolution of the cumulative delta-hedging P&L with 252 time steps using Equation (5.1). Show one path where the final P&L is positive and one path where it is negative.

(b) Using 10,000 simulations, compute the empirical distribution of the final cumulative delta-hedging P&L. What is the average P&L?

5.2   Volatility Trading with Options

(a) You are long a call, which you delta-hedge continuously until maturity. Your cumulative P&L is given by Equation (5.2).

   i. Suppose the "real" stock price process is a geometric Brownian motion with drift μ and realized volatility $\sigma > \sigma^*$. Show that you are guaranteed a positive profit.

   ii. Suppose the "real" stock price process is $dS_t/S_t = \mu_t dt + \sigma_t dW_t$ where μ_t and σ_t are stochastic with $\mathbb{E}_t(\sigma_t^2) > \sigma^{*2}$. Show that your expected P&L (unconditionally from time 0) is positive.

(b) You are long two one-year calls in quantities q_1 and q_2 on two independent underlying stocks, which you delta-hedge continuously until maturity. Suppose that the distributions of the two cumulative P&L equations are normal with means m_1, m_2, and standard deviations s_1, s_2. What is the distribution of the aggregate cumulative P&L of your option book? Show that its standard deviation must be less than $(q_1 + q_2)\max(s_1, s_2)$.

5.3 Fair Variance Swap Strike

Using your SVI calibration results from Problem 2.5 and assuming zero interest rates, estimate the corresponding fair variance swap strike in accordance with Equation (5.3).

5.4 Generalized Variance Swaps

A generalized variance swap has payoff:

$$10,000 \times \left(\frac{252}{N} \sum_{i=0}^{N-1} f(S_i) \ln^2 \frac{S_{i+1}}{S_i} - K_{gvar}^2 \right)$$

where $f(S)$ is a general function of the underlying spot price S, S_t is the spot price at time t, N is the number of trading days until maturity, and K_{gvar} is the strike level. Assume zero interest and dividend rates, and that $dS_t/S_t = \sigma_t dW_t$ under the risk-neutral measure.

(a) Let $g(S) = \int_1^S dy \int_1^y \frac{f(x)}{x^2} dx$. Using the Ito-Doeblin theorem, show that:

$$\int_0^T f(S_t)\sigma_t^2 dt = 2g(S_T) - 2g(S_0) - 2\int_0^T g'(S_t)dS_t$$

What can you infer about the fair value and hedging strategy of generalized variance?

(b) Show that the fair strike is

$$K_{gvar} = \sqrt{ \frac{2}{T} \left(\int_0^{S_0} \frac{f(K)}{K^2} p(K)dK + \int_{S_0}^\infty \frac{f(K)}{K^2} c(K)dK \right) }$$

(c) *Application: corridor variance swap.* What does the formula for the fair strike become in case of the corridor variance swap where daily realized variance only accrues at time t when $L < S_t < U$?

5.5   Call on Realized Variance

Consider the model $dv_t/v_t = 2\omega\frac{T-t}{T}dW_t$ for the forward price at time t of realized variance observed over a fixed period $[0,T]$. In particular, v_T is the terminal historical variance, and $v_0 = \mathbb{E}(v_T)$ is the undiscounted fair strike of a variance swap at time 0.

(a) Show that the price of an at-the-money forward call on realized variance with payoff $\max(0, v_T - v_0)$ is given as:

$$\text{Varcall}_0 = e^{-rT}v_0\left[2N\left(\omega\sqrt{\frac{T}{3}}\right) - 1\right]$$

(b) Using a first-order Taylor expansion show that

$$\text{Varcall}_0 \approx \frac{2}{\sqrt{2\pi}}e^{-rT}v_0\omega\sqrt{\frac{T}{3}}$$

CHAPTER **6**

Introducing Correlation

Correlation is almost as ubiquitous as volatility in quantitative finance. For example the downward-sloping volatility smile observed in equities may be explained by the negative correlation between stock prices and volatility. In this chapter we introduce various measures of correlation between assets, investigate their properties, and present simple multiasset extensions of the Black-Scholes and Local Volatility models.

6-1 MEASURING CORRELATION

Correlation is the degree to which two quantities are linearly associated. A correlation of $+1$ or -1 means that the linear relationship is perfect, while a correlation of 0 typically[1] indicates independence.

There are two kinds of correlation between two financial assets:

1. Historical correlation, based on historical returns;
2. Implied correlation, derived from option prices.

6-1.1 Historical Correlation

Historical correlation between two assets $S^{(1)}$ and $S^{(2)}$ is usually measured as the Pearson's correlation coefficient between their N historical returns observed at regular intervals:

$$\rho^{\dagger}_{1,2} = \frac{\text{Cov}^{\dagger}_{1,2}}{\sigma^{\dagger}_1 \sigma^{\dagger}_2} = \frac{\sum_{i=1}^{N} \left(r_i^{(1)} - \bar{r}^{(1)}\right)\left(r_i^{(2)} - \bar{r}^{(2)}\right)}{\sqrt{\sum_{i=1}^{N} \left(r_i^{(1)} - \bar{r}^{(1)}\right)^2 \times \sum_{i=1}^{N} \left(r_i^{(2)} - \bar{r}^{(2)}\right)^2}}$$

---

[1]Recall that if two random variables X, Y are independent their correlation must be zero; however, the converse is not necessarily true.

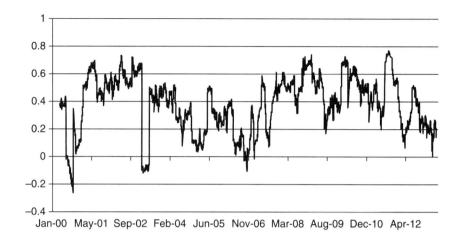

FIGURE 6.1 Historical correlation of daily returns between Apple and Microsoft over a three-month rolling window since 2000.

where $\text{Cov}^\dagger_{1,2}$ is historical covariance, $\sigma^\dagger$'s are historical standard deviations, $r_i^{(j)}$ is the return on asset $S^{(j)}$ for observation i, and $\bar{r}^{(j)} = \frac{1}{N}\sum_{i=1}^{N} r_i^{(j)}$ is the mean return on asset $S^{(j)}$. Returns may be computed on an arithmetic or logarithmic basis; occasionally the mean returns are assumed to be zero.

Figure 6.1 shows the evolution of the historical correlation between Microsoft and Apple over a three-month rolling window since 2000. We can see that this correlation has varied quite significantly over time.

Note that using daily returns can produce misleading results for assets trading within different time zones; in this case it is preferable to estimate correlation using weekly returns. Figure 6.2 compares the two methods for the S&P 500 and Nikkei 225 indexes. We can see that the correlation observed on weekly returns is significantly higher.

6-1.2 Implied Correlation

Implied correlation between two assets $S^{(1)}$ and $S^{(2)}$ is derived from an option price, such as a quote for an over-the-counter (OTC) basket option. Typically the quote is converted into an implied basket volatility σ^*_{Basket} from which implied correlation may be extracted through the formula:

$$\sigma^*_{\text{Basket}} = \sqrt{w_1^2\sigma_1^{*2} + w_2^2\sigma_2^{*2} + 2w_1 w_2\sigma_1^*\sigma_2^*\rho_{1,2}^*}, \text{ that is,}$$

$$\rho_{1,2}^* = \frac{\sigma^{*2}_{\text{Basket}} - w_1^2\sigma_1^{*2} - w_2^2\sigma_2^{*2}}{2w_1 w_2\sigma_1^*\sigma_2^*} = \frac{\sigma^{*2}_{\text{Basket}} - (w_1^2\sigma_1^{*2} + w_2^2\sigma_2^{*2})}{(w_1\sigma_1^* + w_2\sigma_2^*)^2 - (w_1^2\sigma_1^{*2} + w_2^2\sigma_2^{*2})}$$

where w_j is the weight on asset $S^{(j)}$ and σ_j^* is the implied volatility of asset $S^{(j)}$.

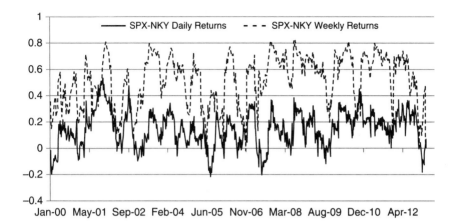

FIGURE 6.2 Historical correlation of daily and weekly returns between S&P 500 and Nikkei 225 over a three-month rolling window since 2000.

Conventionally all implied volatilities are for the same moneyness level k (strike over spot) and maturity T, and weights are equal.

6-2 CORRELATION MATRICES

Very often we are interested in correlation for a selection of $n \geq 2$ assets. This leads to a correlation matrix of the form:

$$
R = \begin{pmatrix}
1 & \rho_{1,2} & \rho_{1,3} & \cdots & \rho_{1,n} \\
\rho_{2,1} & 1 & \rho_{2,3} & \cdots & \rho_{2,n} \\
\rho_{3,1} & \rho_{3,2} & 1 & \cdots & \rho_{3,n} \\
\vdots & \vdots & \vdots & \ddots & \vdots \\
\rho_{n,1} & \rho_{n,2} & \rho_{n,3} & \cdots & 1
\end{pmatrix}
$$

where $\rho_{i,j}$ is the pairwise correlation coefficient between assets $S^{(i)}$ and $S^{(j)}$, which may either be historical or implied. Note that R is symmetric because $\rho_{i,j} = \rho_{j,i}$.

Not every symmetric matrix with entries in $[-1, 1]$ and a diagonal of 1's is a candidate for a correlation matrix R. This is because the correlation between assets $S^{(i)}$ and $S^{(j)}$ and assets $S^{(j)}$ and $S^{(k)}$ says something about the correlation between assets $S^{(i)}$ and $S^{(k)}$—intuitively, if Microsoft and Apple are highly correlated, and Apple and IBM are also highly correlated, then Microsoft and IBM must also have some positive correlation.

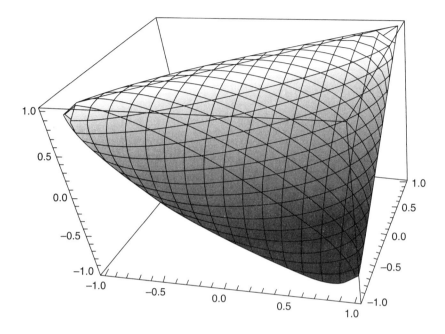

FIGURE 6.3 Envelope of admissible correlation values when $n = 3$.

Figure 6.3 shows the envelope of admissible correlation values when $n = 3$. We can see that certain regions, such as around the corner $(-1, -1, -1)$ are not admissible.

Specifically, correlation matrices must be positive-semidefinite; that is, their eigenvalues must all be nonnegative. This property is always verified for historical correlation but not necessarily for implied correlation. Additionally the sum of all eigenvalues must equal the trace, that is, n.

A common fix for an indefinite candidate matrix M is to replace its negative eigenvalues with zeros and adjust its positive eigenvalues to maintain a sum of n:

$$R = \Omega D_{adj}\Omega^{T}$$

where Ω is the orthogonal matrix of eigenvectors of M with eigenvalues $(\lambda_1, \ldots, \lambda_n)$ and D_{adj} is the diagonal matrix of adjusted eigenvalues with entries $\lambda_i^{adj} = \frac{\lambda_i^+}{\sum_{j=1}^{n} \lambda_j^+}$. Alternatively one may use the method proposed by Higham (2002).

In equities correlation matrices have other empirical properties. Plerou et al. (2002) and Potters, Bouchaud, and Laloux (2005) found for U.S. stocks that the top eigenvalue typically dominates all the other ones. Furthermore, the corresponding eigenvector is more or less an equally weighted portfolio of all the stocks. This suggests that one factor ("the market") strongly drives the behavior of each stock.

6-3 CORRELATION AVERAGE

To summarize the overall level of correlation across n assets, it is common practice to compute the average of the correlation matrix, excluding the diagonal of 1's. The formula for a given weighting vector x is then:

$$\rho(x) = \frac{\sum_{i<j} x_i x_j \rho_{i,j}}{\sum_{i<j} x_i x_j} = \frac{x^T R x - x^T x}{(x^T e)^2 - x^T x} \tag{6.1}$$

where e is the vector of 1's. In the main case of interest where all the weights are nonnegative we have:

$$-1 \le -\frac{x^T x}{(x^T e)^2 - x^T x} \le \rho(x) \le (n-1)\frac{x^T x}{(x^T e)^2 - x^T x} \le 1$$

but in general $\rho(x)$ could lie outside of these bounds. In practice, when applying sensible weights to a large equity correlation matrix, $\rho(x)$ can safely be assumed to be positive.

Common choices for x are:

- Equal weights: $x = e$. In this case the average correlation formula simplifies to:

$$\rho(e) = \frac{2}{n(n-1)} \sum_{i<j} \rho_{i,j}$$

and we have the bounds:

$$-\frac{1}{n-1} \le \rho(e) \le 1$$

- Market capitalization weights: $x = w$. This is particularly relevant when the n stocks are the constituents of an equity index such as the S&P 500.

- Volatility and market capitalization weights: $x = (w_1\sigma_1, \ldots, w_n\sigma_n)^T$, where σ's may either be historical or implied volatilities. This case is particularly appealing because of the identity[2] or shortcut formula:

$$\rho \begin{pmatrix} w_1\sigma_1 \\ \vdots \\ w_n\sigma_n \end{pmatrix} = \frac{\sigma_{\text{Basket}}^2 - \sum_{i=1}^{n} w_i^2\sigma_i^2}{\left(\sum_{i=1}^{n} w_i\sigma_i\right)^2 - \sum_{i=1}^{n} w_i^2\sigma_i^2}$$

where σ_{Basket} is the volatility of the all-stock portfolio with weights w. Assimilating an equity index to a portfolio of stocks with fixed weights,[3] this formula allows us to compute the average implied correlation using only listed option prices.

In practice, for large baskets ($n > 30$), these various choices for x tend to produce similar results within a few correlation points, as observed by Tierens and Anadu (2004) and illustrated in Figure 6.4.

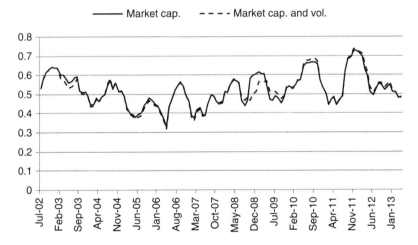

FIGURE 6.4 Realized average correlation for the EuroStoxx 50 index over a six-month rolling window using market capitalization weights and volatility and market capitalization weights.

---

[2]Note that the identity is exact for arithmetic returns but only approximate for logarithmic returns.

[3]Note that in reality equity index weights continuously change with stock prices. However, these variations tend to be limited, especially over short time horizons.

6-3.1   Correlation Proxy

Equation (6.1) is related to a mathematical quantity known as the Rayleigh quotient $\mathfrak{R}(x) = \frac{x^T R x}{x^T x}$; specifically, dividing both numerator and denominator by $n x^T x = (x^T x)(e^T e)$:

$$\rho(x) = \frac{\frac{1}{n}\mathfrak{R}(x) - \frac{1}{n}}{\frac{(x^T e)^2}{(x^T x)(e^T e)} - \frac{1}{n}} = \frac{\frac{1}{n}\mathfrak{R}(x) - \frac{1}{n}}{\cos^2\theta - \frac{1}{n}}$$

where θ is the angle between vectors x and e.

As $n \to \infty$ we have the proxy formula:

$$\rho(x) \sim \frac{\frac{1}{n}\mathfrak{R}(x)}{\cos^2\theta} = \frac{x^T R x}{(x^T e)^2}$$

subject to certain technical conditions, which are met in practice. In particular, for volatility and market capitalization weights, the proxy formula equates the now well-known squared ratio of basket volatility to average stock volatility:

$$\rho(x) \sim \left(\frac{\sigma_{\text{Basket}}}{\sum_i w_i \sigma_i} \right)^2$$

FOCUS ON THE PROXY FORMULA

It is easy to establish the proxy formula when all correlation coefficients are positive (see, e.g., Bossu and Henrotte (2012)). However, when some correlation coefficients are negative we must use a more elaborate proof. Specifically, using the spectral decomposition of R, we may write:

$$\mathfrak{R}(x) = \sum_{i=1}^{n} \lambda_i \frac{(x^T v_i)^2}{(x^T x)(v_i^T v_i)}$$

where v's form an orthogonal basis of eigenvectors and λ's are their associated eigenvalues.

Therefore $\mathfrak{R}(x) \geq \sum\limits_{i=1}^{n} \lambda_i \min\limits_{1 \leq j \leq n} \dfrac{(x^T v_j)^2}{(x^T x)(v_j^T v_j)} = n \min\limits_{1 \leq j \leq n} \dfrac{(x^T v_j)^2}{(x^T x)(v_j^T v_j)}$ since all eigenvalues must sum to n. Assuming that x is never orthogonal to any eigenvector v_i (also in the limit) then $\mathfrak{R}(x) \to \infty$ and thus $\frac{1}{n}\mathfrak{R}(x) - \frac{1}{n} \sim \frac{1}{n}\mathfrak{R}(x)$. Furthermore, if x is also never orthogonal to e (also in the limit) then $\cos^2\theta - \frac{1}{n} \sim \cos^2\theta$, which completes the proof that $\rho(x) \sim \dfrac{\frac{1}{n}\mathfrak{R}(x)}{\cos^2\theta} = \dfrac{x^T R x}{(x^T e)^2}$.

6-3.2 Some Properties of the Correlation Proxy

We now focus on some fundamental properties of the proxy formula $\hat{\rho}(x) = \dfrac{x^T R x}{(x^T e)^2}$. In what follows it is assumed that the eigenvalues of R are sorted by ascending order.

First, a property of the Rayleigh quotient is that it must be comprised between the top and bottom eigenvalues, which implies that:

$$0 \leq \frac{\lambda_1/n}{\cos^2\theta} \leq \hat{\rho}(x) \leq \frac{\lambda_n/n}{\cos^2\theta} \leq \frac{1}{\cos^2\theta}$$

Note that the lower bound $\frac{\lambda_1/n}{\cos^2\theta}$ can be slightly improved in the unconstrained case (see Problem 6.1) and that tighter numerical bounds can be computed through quadratic optimization methods in the constrained case where $x \geq 0$.

Second, another quantity of interest is the distance between two average correlation measures $\Delta = |\hat{\rho}(x) - \hat{\rho}(y)|$. Restricting ourselves to vectors x and y such that $x^T e = y^T e = 1$ we may rewrite without loss of generality:

$$\Delta = \left| x^T R x - y^T R y \right| = \left| (x + y)^T R(x - y) \right|$$

The Cauchy-Schwarz inequality then gives the general upper bound $\Delta \leq \lambda_n \|x + y\| \|x - y\|$ but in practice it is not satisfactory. To find a better upper bound we must look at the spectral decomposition of R:

$$R = \sum_{i=1}^{n} \lambda_i \frac{v_i v_i^T}{v_i^T v_i}$$

where v_i is an eigenvector with associated eigenvalue λ_i. Thus, for any vectors a and b:

$$\frac{a^T R b}{\sqrt{a^T a \ b^T b}} = \sum_{i=1}^{n} \lambda_i \frac{a^T v_i}{\sqrt{a^T a \ v_i^T v_i}} \frac{v_i^T b}{\sqrt{v_i^T v_i \ b^T b}} = \sum_{i=1}^{n} \lambda_i \cos \widehat{(a, v_i)} \cos \widehat{(v_i, b)}$$

where $\widehat{(u, v)}$ denotes the absolute angle in $[0, \pi]$ between any two vectors u and v.

Recalling that the top eigenvalue of stock correlation matrices dominates all other eigenvalues, we are induced to split the sum accordingly:

$$\frac{a^T R b}{\sqrt{a^T a \ b^T b}} = \sum_{i=1}^{n-1} \lambda_i \cos \widehat{(a, v_i)} \cos \widehat{(v_i, b)} + \lambda_n \cos \widehat{(a, v_n)} \cos \widehat{(v_n, b)}$$

Furthermore $\cos \alpha \cos \beta = \cos(\alpha + \beta) + \sin \alpha \sin \beta$, so that:

$$\frac{a^T R b}{\sqrt{a^T a \ b^T b}} = \sum_{i=1}^{n-1} \lambda_i \cos \widehat{(a, v_i)} \cos \widehat{(v_i, b)} + \lambda_n \sin \widehat{(a, v_n)} \sin \widehat{(v_n, b)}$$
$$+ \lambda_n \cos[\widehat{(a, v_n)} + \widehat{(v_n, b)}]$$

We now invoke the fifth property of the Euclidean metric[4] to get $|\cos \widehat{(a, v_i)}| \leq \sin \widehat{(a, v_n)}$, $|\cos \widehat{(v_i, b)}| \leq \sin \widehat{(v_n, b)}$ and for $\widehat{(a, v_n)} + \widehat{(v_n, b)} \leq \frac{\pi}{2}$: $0 \leq \cos[\widehat{(a, v_n)} + \widehat{(v_n, b)}] \leq \cos \widehat{(a, b)}$, so that:

$$\left| \frac{a^T R b}{\sqrt{a^T a \ b^T b}} \right| \leq n \sin \widehat{(a, v_n)} \sin \widehat{(v_n, b)} + \lambda_n \cos \widehat{(a, b)}$$

because the eigenvalues sum to n.

Taking $a = x + y$, $b = x - y$ and rearranging terms we get:

$$\Delta \leq n\|x + y\|\|x - y\| \left[\sin \widehat{(x + y, v_n)} \sin \widehat{(v_n, x - y)} + \frac{\lambda_n}{n} \cos \widehat{(x + y, x - y)} \right]$$

---

[4]See Dattorro (2008) who cites Blumenthal (1933). See also Laurence et al. (2008) who cite De Finetti (1937).

In practice the quantity between brackets is usually small because x, y are "close" to v_n and $x + y$, $x - y$ are nearly orthogonal.

FOCUS ON THE FIFTH PROPERTY

The fifth property of the Euclidean metric is a triangle inequality for angles in three dimensions, which is surprisingly not documented in mainstream geometry textbooks. Specifically it states that for any three vectors u, v, and w we have:

$$|\widehat{(u,v)} - \widehat{(v,w)}| \leq \widehat{(u,w)} \leq \widehat{(u,v)} + \widehat{(v,w)}$$

where all angles are measured between 0 and π. Taking cosines we equivalently have:

$$\cos[\widehat{(u,v)} + \widehat{(v,w)}] \leq \cos\widehat{(u,w)} \leq \cos[\widehat{(u,v)} - \widehat{(v,w)}].$$

As a corollary if e.g. $\widehat{(v,w)} = \pi/2$ then $|\cos\widehat{(u,w)}| \leq \cos\left(\frac{\pi}{2} - \widehat{(u,v)}\right)$
$= \sin\widehat{(u,v)}$

6-4 BLACK-SCHOLES WITH CONSTANT CORRELATION

Extending Black-Scholes to a basket of n underlying assets $S^{(1)}, \ldots, S^{(n)}$ with constant correlation is fairly straightforward, except perhaps notation-wise.

Given a vector of volatilities $(\sigma_1, \ldots, \sigma_n)$ and a correlation matrix $(\rho_{i,j})$, assume that the prices of the underlying assets follow n correlated geometric Brownian motions:

$$dS_t^{(1)} = \mu_1 S_t^{(1)} dt + \sigma_1 S_t^{(1)} dW_t^{(1)}$$
$$dS_t^{(2)} = \mu_2 S_t^{(2)} dt + \sigma_2 S_t^{(2)} dW_t^{(2)}$$
$$\vdots$$
$$dS_t^{(n)} = \mu_n S_t^{(n)} dt + \sigma_n S_t^{(n)} dW_t^{(n)}$$

where $dW_t^{(i)} dW_t^{(j)} \equiv \rho_{i,j} dt$. If the derivative's value only depends on time and the n spot prices, we have $D_t = f(t, S_t^{(1)}, \ldots, S_t^{(n)})$ and we can apply the multidimensional version of the Ito-Doeblin theorem to get:

$$dD_t = df = \frac{\partial f}{\partial t} dt + \sum_{i=1}^{n} \frac{\partial f}{\partial S^{(i)}} dS_t^{(i)} + \frac{1}{2} \sum_{i=1}^{n} \sum_{j=1}^{n} \frac{\partial^2 f}{\partial S^{(i)} \partial S^{(j)}} \sigma_i \sigma_j \rho_{i,j} S_t^{(i)} S_t^{(j)} dt$$

$$= \frac{\partial f}{\partial t} dt + \nabla f^T dS_t + \frac{1}{2} dS_t^T \nabla^2 f \, dS_t$$

where ∇f and $\nabla^2 f$ are the gradient and Hessian of f, respectively.

A portfolio long one unit of derivative and short $\delta_i = \frac{\partial f}{\partial S^{(i)}}$ units of each asset $S^{(i)}$ is then riskless, and by the same reasoning as in the single-asset case we obtain a multidimensional partial differential equation for f whose only parameters are the interest rate r, the volatility vector and the correlation matrix:

$$rf = \frac{\partial f}{\partial t} + r \sum_{i=1}^{n} \frac{\partial f}{\partial S^{(i)}} S_t^{(i)} + \frac{1}{2} \sum_{i=1}^{n} \sum_{j=1}^{n} \frac{\partial^2 f}{\partial S^{(i)} \partial S^{(j)}} \sigma_i \sigma_j \rho_{i,j} S_t^{(i)} S_t^{(j)}$$

Solving partial differential equations in high dimension is very hard mathematically and computationally. In practice, the numerical method of choice to implement the multiasset Black-Scholes model is Monte Carlo simulation under the risk-neutral measure. The Cholesky decomposition of the correlation matrix is then typically used to generate correlated Brownian motions from uncorrelated ones.

FOCUS ON THE CHOLESKY DECOMPOSITION

The Cholesky decomposition of a symmetric, positive-definite matrix A is the lower triangular matrix C with strictly positive diagonal entries such that $A = CC^T$. It can be computed with a short algorithm of complexity $O(n^3)$.

The Cholesky decomposition C of a correlation matrix R may be used to generate correlated standard normals $Y = XC^T$ from a sample X of uncorrelated ones with m rows and n columns. Indeed the covariance estimate for Y up to a multiplicative factor is:

$$Y^T Y = CX^T XC^T \approx CC^T = R$$

where we used $X^T X \approx I$, which is true for large m.

6-5 LOCAL VOLATILITY WITH CONSTANT CORRELATION

Another straightforward extension of a popular model is local volatility with constant correlation (LVCC). Keeping the notations of Section 6-4, this model assumes dynamics of the form:

$$dS_t^{(1)} = \mu_1 S_t^{(1)} dt + \sigma_1^{\text{loc}}(t, S_t^{(1)}) S_t^{(1)} dW_t^{(1)}$$
$$dS_t^{(2)} = \mu_2 S_t^{(2)} dt + \sigma_2^{\text{loc}}(t, S_t^{(2)}) S_t^{(2)} dW_t^{(2)}$$
$$\vdots$$
$$dS_t^{(n)} = \mu_n S_t^{(n)} dt + \sigma_n^{\text{loc}}(t, S_t^{(n)}) S_t^{(n)} dW_t^{(n)}$$

where $\sigma_i^{\text{loc}}(t, S)$ is the local volatility function for asset $S^{(i)}$ (see Chapter 4) and $dW_t^{(i)} dW_t^{(j)} \equiv \rho_{i,j} dt$ as before.

The same reasoning as in Section 6-4 then applies, with identical results after substituting local volatilities. Again Monte Carlo simulations are overwhelmingly preferred to other numerical methods such as multidimensional binomial trees or finite difference lattices.

Until recently the local volatility model with constant correlation was widely used to price a broad range of multiasset exotic options. In Chapter 8, we introduce the next generation of models where correlation is allowed to vary.

REFERENCES

Blumenthal, Leonard M. 1933. "On the four-point property." *Bulletin of the American Mathematical Society*, 39: 423–426.

Bossu, Sébastien, and Philippe Henrotte. 2012. *An Introduction to Equity Derivatives: Theory and Practice*, 2nd ed. Chichester, UK: John Wiley & Sons.

Dattorro, Jon. 2008. *Convex Optimization & Euclidean Distance Geometry*. Palo Alto, CA: Meboo Publishing USA.

De Finetti, Bruno. 1937. "A proposito di correlazione." *Supplemento Statistico ai Nuovi problemi di Politica, Storia ed Economia*, 3: 41–57. English translation in Laurence et al. (2008).

Higham, Nicholas J. 2002. "Computing the Nearest Correlation Matrix—A Problem from Finance." *IMA Journal of Numerical Analysis* 22: 329–343.

Laurence, Peter, Tai-Ho Hwang, and Luca Barone. 2008. "Geometric Properties of Multivariate Correlation in de Finetti's Approach to Insurance Theory." *Electronic Journal for History of Probability and Statistics* 4(2).

Plerou, Vasiliki, Parameswaran Gopikrishnan, Bernd Rosenow, Luis A. Nunes Ama-
ral, Thomas Guhr, and H. Eugene Stanley. 2002. "Random Matrix Approach
to Cross Correlations in Financial Data." *Physical Review E* 65: 1–18.

Potters, Marc, Jean-Philippe Bouchaud, and Laurent Laloux. 2005. "Financial Applications of Random Matrix Theory: Old Laces and New Pieces." *Acta Physica
Polonica B* (36): 2767–2784.

Tierens, Ingrid, and Margaret Anadu. 2004. "Does It Matter Which Methodology
You Use to Measure Average Correlation across Stocks?" Goldman Sachs Equity
Derivatives Strategy report, April 2004.

PROBLEMS

6.1   Lower Bound for Average Correlation

Let R be a $n \times n$ correlation matrix. For any $n \times n$ positive-definite matrix A
define $\hat{\rho}_A(x) = \frac{x^T A x}{(x^T e)^2}$ where e is the vector of 1's and x is an arbitrary vector
which is nonorthogonal to e.

(a) Show that $\hat{\rho}_R(e) \leq \frac{1}{n}\lambda_n$ where λ_n is the top eigenvalue of R.

(b) Show that $\hat{\rho}_R(x) \geq \left[\hat{\rho}_{R^{-1}}(e)\right]^{-1}$. *Hint: This can be formulated as a
constrained optimization problem and solved with; for example, the
Lagrangian method.*

(c) We want to approximate the distance $d = \hat{\rho}_R(e) - [\hat{\rho}_{R^{-1}}(e)]^{-1}$ when R
is an equity correlation matrix with top eigenvalue $\lambda_n \gg \lambda_{n-1}$ and the
corresponding top eigenvector v_n is an all-stock portfolio close to e/n (up
to a scaling factor).

   i.   Show that d may be rewritten as $d = \frac{1}{n}(A - H)$ where A, H are
        respectively the arithmetic and harmonic weighted averages of the
        eigenvalues of R, with weights $\alpha_i = \cos^2(\widehat{e, v_i})$. *Hint: Use Parseval's
        identity to show that $\sum_{i=1}^{n} \alpha_i = 1$.*

   ii. Argue that $d \approx \left[\frac{1-\alpha_n}{n-1}\left(1 - \frac{\lambda_n}{n}\right) + \alpha_n \frac{\lambda_n}{n}\right] - \frac{1}{\frac{1-\alpha_n}{n-1}\sum_{i=1}^{n-1}\frac{n}{\lambda_i} + \alpha_n \frac{n}{\lambda_n}}$

6.2   Geometric Basket Call

Consider a call option with payoff $\max(0, b_T - k)$ on a geometric basket
calculated as $b_T = \prod_{i=1}^{n} \left(\frac{S_T^{(i)}}{S_0^{(i)}}\right)^{w_i}$ where $S_t^{(i)}$ is the price of the underlying asset
$S^{(i)}$ at time t and the nonnegative basket weights (w_i) sum to 1.

(a) In the Black-Scholes model with constant correlation, show that under the risk-neutral measure b_T is lognormally distributed and find the distribution parameters as functions of volatilities and correlations.
(b) Find a closed-form formula for the price of the call.

6.3 Worst-Of Put Pricing

Using the Black-Scholes model with constant correlation and Monte Carlo simulations, calculate the price of a one-year at-the-money worst-of put option (see Section 1-2.3) on Apple, Microsoft, and Google, in accordance with the following parameters:

- Interest rate: 1%
- Dividend rates: Apple 3%, Microsoft 2.8%, Google 0%
- Volatilities: Apple 30%, Microsoft 26%, Google 23%
- Correlations: Apple-Google: 35%, Apple-Microsoft: 30%, Google-Microsoft: 50%

6.4 Continuously Monitored Correlation

Consider the LVCC model for two assets $S^{(1)}$ and $S^{(2)}$. Define the continuously monitored realized correlation coefficient as:

$$c = \frac{\int_0^T \frac{dS_t^{(1)}}{S_t^{(1)}} \frac{dS_t^{(2)}}{S_t^{(2)}}}{\sqrt{\int_0^T \left[\frac{dS_t^{(1)}}{S_t^{(1)}}\right]^2 \times \int_0^T \left[\frac{dS_t^{(2)}}{S_t^{(2)}}\right]^2}}.$$

Show that $c \le \rho_{1,2}$

CHAPTER 7

Correlation Trading

With the development of multiasset exotic products it became possible, and at times necessary, to trade correlation more or less directly. The first correlation trades were actually dispersion trades where a long or short position on a multi-asset option is offset by a reverse position on single-asset options. Recently pure correlation trades appeared in the form of correlation swaps.

7-1   DISPERSION TRADING

The payoff of a dispersion trade is of the form:

$$\text{Basket Option Payoff} - \beta \times \sum_i \text{Weight}_i \times \text{Single Option Payoff}_i$$

where β is an arbitrary coefficient or leg ratio, which is typically determined so that the trade has zero initial cost, and all other notations are self-explanatory.

The intuition behind dispersion trades is that the basket option's leg provides exposure to volatility and correlation. To isolate the correlation exposure, it is necessary to hedge, if only approximately, the volatility exposure: this is precisely the purpose of the short single options' leg.

The two most popular types of dispersion trades are *vanilla dispersions*, based on vanilla options (typically straddles), and *variance dispersions*, based on variance swaps.

7-1.1   Vanilla Dispersion Trades

The payoff formula for a vanilla dispersion trade on a selection of n stocks $S^{(1)}, \ldots, S^{(n)}$ with weights $w_1, \ldots, w_n$ is given as:

$$\left| \sum_{i=1}^{n} w_i \frac{S_T^{(i)}}{S_0^{(i)}} - k \right| - \beta \sum_{i=1}^{n} w_i \left| \frac{S_T^{(i)}}{S_0^{(i)}} - k \right|$$

where β is the leg ratio, T is the maturity, and k is the moneyness level (strike/spot).

The trade cost is $\text{Straddle}_0^{\text{Basket}}(k, T) - \beta \sum_{i=1}^{n} w_i \text{Straddle}_0^{(i)}(k, T)$, and the leg ratio for a zero-cost trade is thus $\beta_0 = \dfrac{\text{Straddle}_0^{\text{Basket}}}{\sum_{i=1}^{n} w_i \times \text{Straddle}_0^{(i)}}$. In the case of short-term near-the-money forward straddles, we have the proxy $\beta_0 \approx \dfrac{\sigma_{\text{Basket}}^*}{\sum_{i=1}^{n} w_i \sigma_i^*} \approx \sqrt{\rho_{\text{ATM}}^*}$ where σ^*'s are at-the-money implied volatilities and ρ_{ATM}^* is at-the-money average implied correlation (see Problem 7.1).

From a trading perspective, vanilla dispersion trades are attractive because they tend to be liquid, cost-effective, and customizable. However, a major disadvantage is that they need to be delta-hedged; furthermore, the delta-hedging profit and loss (P&L) involves the gammas of $n + 1$ options and is only very loosely connected to correlation:

- Assuming constant implied volatility and zero interest rates, the total delta-hedging P&L for option i (where $i = $ Basket or $1, \dots, n$) is:

$$\int_0^T \Gamma_{t,i}^{\$}(\sigma_{t,i}^2 - \sigma_i^{*2})dt$$

where $\Gamma_{t,i}^{\$} = \frac{1}{2}\Gamma_{t,i}S_{t,i}^2$ is the option's dollar gamma at time t, $\sigma_{t,i}$ is the instantaneous volatility of asset $S^{(i)}$ at time t, and σ_i^* is implied volatility.

- The total delta-hedging P&L of the dispersion trade is thus:

$$\text{Dispersion P\&L} = \int_0^T \left[\Gamma_{t,\text{Basket}}^{\$} \left(\sigma_{t,\text{Basket}}^2 - \sigma_{\text{Basket}}^{*2} \right) \right.$$
$$\left. - \beta \sum_{i=1}^{n} w_i \Gamma_{t,i}^{\$} \left(\sigma_{t,i}^2 - \sigma_i^{*2} \right) \right] dt$$

Using the proxy formula from Section 6-3.1 and rearranging terms we can write:

$$\text{Dispersion P\&L} \approx \int_0^T \left[\Gamma_{t,\text{Basket}}^{\$} \hat{\rho}_t \bar{\sigma}_t^2 - \beta \sum_{i=1}^{n} w_i \Gamma_{t,i}^{\$} \sigma_{t,i}^2 \right] dt$$
$$- \int_0^T \left[\Gamma_{t,\text{Basket}}^{\$} \hat{\rho}^* \bar{\sigma}^{*2} - \beta \sum_{i=1}^{n} w_i \Gamma_{t,i}^{\$} \sigma_i^{*2} \right] dt$$

Because the dollar gammas are all different and keep changing, the single option leg will likely be a poorly efficient hedge against the volatility exposure resulting from $\bar{\sigma}_t$.

7-1.2 Variance Dispersion Trades

Variance dispersion trades appeared as a spinoff of the expansion of the variance swaps market and offer a much more direct way to trade correlation than vanilla dispersions. Specifically, the payoff formula for a selection of n stocks $S^{(1)}, \ldots, S^{(n)}$ with weights $w_1, \ldots, w_n$ is:

$$\sigma^2_{\text{Basket}} - \beta \sum_{i=1}^{n} w_i \sigma_i^2$$

where σ's are realized volatilities between the start date $t = 0$ and the maturity date $t = T$ and β is the leg ratio. Typically the n stocks are the constituents of an equity index (or a subset), the weights are based on market capitalization at the start date, and σ_{Basket} is replaced with the volatility of the index. In practice each realized volatility is capped at a certain level to mitigate volatility "explosions" resulting from bankruptcies, for example.

The trade cost is simply $\sigma^{\star 2}_{\text{Basket}} - \beta \sum_{i=1}^{n} w_i \sigma_i^{\star 2}$ where $\sigma^\star$'s are fair variance swap strikes, and thus the leg ratio for a zero-cost trade is $\beta_0 = \dfrac{\sigma^{\star 2}_{\text{Basket}}}{\sum_{i=1}^{n} w_i \sigma_i^{\star 2}}$. Note that β_0 differs slightly from the correlation proxy formula $\hat{\rho}^\star = \dfrac{\sigma^{\star 2}_{\text{Basket}}}{\left(\sum_{i=1}^{n} w_i \sigma_i^\star \right)^2}$ and gives rise to a new average correlation measure:

$$\hat{\rho}(w, \sigma) = \hat{\rho} \begin{pmatrix} w_1 \sigma_1 \\ \vdots \\ w_n \sigma_n \end{pmatrix} \times \frac{\left(\sum_{i=1}^{n} w_i \sigma_i \right)^2}{\sum_{i=1}^{n} w_i \sigma_i^2}.$$

Note that by Jensen's inequality we must have $\hat{\rho} \le \hat{\rho}$. Figure 7.1 shows that $\hat{\rho}^\star, \hat{\rho}^\star$ differ very little in practice, and that they are somewhat above at-the-money implied correlation $\hat{\rho}^*_{\text{ATM}}$.

By definition of $\hat{\rho}$ we may rewrite the payoff of a zero-cost variance dispersion trade as:

$$(\hat{\rho} - \hat{\rho}^\star) \sum_{i=1}^{n} w_i \sigma_i^2$$

In other words the P&L on a zero-cost variance dispersion trade is the spread between realized and implied average correlation multiplied by the average realized variance of the constituent stocks. As such the trade will make money when realized correlation exceeds implied correlation, and lose money otherwise—a remarkable property.

From a trading perspective, variance dispersion trades are attractive because there is a persistent gap between implied and realized correlation as shown in Figure 7.2 on the Dow Jones EuroStoxx50 index.

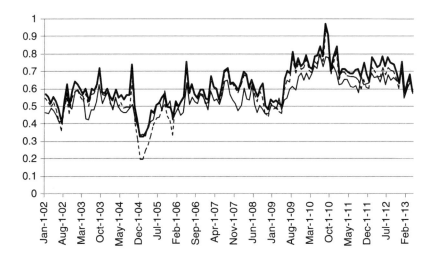

FIGURE 7.1 Comparison between the six-month implied correlation proxy $\widehat{\rho}^*$ (bold line), the six-month variance-based implied correlation $\widehat{\rho}^\star$ (dashed line), and at-the-money implied correlation $\widehat{\rho}^*_{\text{ATM}}$ (thin line) for the Dow Jones EuroStoxx 50 index.
Data source: OptionMetrics.

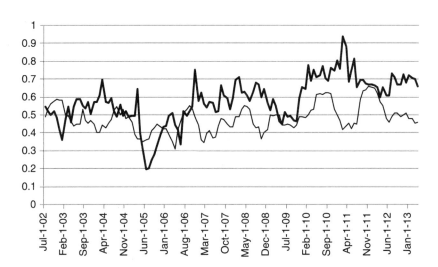

FIGURE 7.2 Six-month variance-based implied correlation $\widehat{\rho}^\star$ (bold line) and realized correlation $\widehat{\rho}$ six months later (thin line) for the Dow Jones EuroStoxx 50 index.
Data sources: OptionMetrics, Bloomberg.

FOCUS ON CROSS-SECTIONAL DISPERSION

The cross-sectional dispersion of n random variables $X_1, \ldots, X_n$ is defined as their average squared deviation from the mean:

$$D = \frac{1}{n} \sum_{i=1}^{n} \left(X_i - \overline{X} \right)^2 = \frac{1}{n} \sum_{i=1}^{n} X_i^2 - \overline{X}^2$$

where $\overline{X} = \frac{1}{n} \sum_{j=1}^{n} X_j$

When dealing with time series such as stock returns we may compute their cross-sectional dispersion through time: $D_t = \frac{1}{n} \sum_{i=1}^{n} (X_{i,t} - \overline{X}_t)^2$. It then turns out that the average cross-sectional dispersion $\overline{D}$ over m time periods matches the payoff of an equally weighted short variance dispersion trade with leg ratio $\beta = 1$, as shown below:

$$\overline{D} = \frac{1}{m} \sum_{t=1}^{m} D_t = \frac{1}{n} \sum_{i=1}^{n} \underbrace{\frac{1}{m} \sum_{t=1}^{m} X_{i,t}^2}_{\sigma_i^2} - \underbrace{\frac{1}{m} \sum_{t=1}^{m} \overline{X}_t^2}_{\sigma_{\text{Basket}}^2}$$

7-2   CORRELATION SWAPS

7-2.1   Payoff

A correlation swap is a forward contract on average realized correlation. Specifically the payoff formula for a selection of n stocks $S^{(1)}, \ldots, S^{(n)}$ with weights $w_1, \ldots, w_n$ is:

$$\frac{\sum\limits_{i<j} w_i w_j \rho_{i,j}}{\sum\limits_{i<j} w_i w_j} - K_{\text{correl}}$$

where ρ's are pairwise correlation coefficients observed between the start date $t = 0$ and the maturity date $t = T$, and K_{correl} is the strike level between 0 and 1. We recognize the average correlation measure $\rho(w)$ from Section 6-3.

The main attraction of correlation swaps is that they are pure correlation trades. The main disadvantage is that there is no consensus model to price and hedge them—in particular the strike K_{correl} trading on the over-the-counter market may significantly differ from average implied correlation measures.

Correlation swaps are typically offered by investment banks to sophisticated investors on an opportunistic basis to offload the correlation risk accumulated by their exotic trading desks. This is because exotic derivatives sold by banks tend to be long correlation (i.e., their value increases when correlation increases), resulting in large short correlation exposures (i.e., the bank loses money when correlation increases).

7-2.2 Pricing

To approach the pricing of correlation swaps, note that when the stocks are the constituents of an equity index and weights are based on market capitalizations, the average realized correlation measure $\rho(w)$ is usually close

to $\rho \begin{pmatrix} w_1\sigma_1 \\ \vdots \\ w_n\sigma_n \end{pmatrix} = \dfrac{\sigma_{\text{Basket}}^2 - \sum_{i=1}^n w_i^2\sigma_i^2}{\left(\sum_{i=1}^n w_i\sigma_i\right)^2 - \sum_{i=1}^n w_i^2\sigma_i^2} \sim \dfrac{\sigma_{\text{Basket}}^2}{\left(\sum_{i=1}^n w_i\sigma_i\right)^2}$, which itself may

be approximated with $\widehat{\rho}(w,\sigma) = \dfrac{\sigma_{\text{Basket}}^2}{\sum_{i=1}^n w_i\sigma_i^2}$. This suggests that a correlation

swap may be approximately priced as a derivative of two tradable assets: basket variance and average constituent variance.

Based on this observation, Bossu (2005) proposed a simple "toy model" to price and hedge correlation swaps, which is a straightforward extension of the Black-Scholes model in the two-asset case. One important theoretical limitation of the toy model is that it is not entirely well-specified and allows average realized correlation to exceed 1 in a small number of paths.

A modified version of the toy model where correlation is constrained between -1 and 1 is derived in Chapter 9. This version is more mathematically satisfying but unfortunately loses the simplicity of the original toy model.

7-2.3 Hedging

While research for the ultimate correlation swap model is still ongoing, we may state certain interesting properties. In general, two-asset models will produce a forward price formula $f_t(X_t, Y_t)$ for correlation where X_t, Y_t are the forward prices at time t of σ_{Basket}^2, $\sum_{i=1}^n w_i\sigma_i^2$ respectively (in particular $X_0 = \sigma_{\text{Basket}}^{\star 2}$, $Y_0 = \sum_{i=1}^n w_i\sigma_i^{\star 2}$, and $X_T = \sigma_{\text{Basket}}^2$, $Y_T = \sum_{i=1}^n w_i\sigma_i^2$). The hedge ratios are then given as $\frac{\partial f}{\partial X}$, $\frac{\partial f}{\partial Y}$ as usual.

Because $f_t(X_t, Y_t) = \mathbb{E}_t\left(\frac{X_T}{Y_T}\right)$ under the forward-neutral measure and because X_T/Y_T is invariant when multiplying X_T and Y_T by the same scalar λ, we must also have $f_t(\lambda X_t, \lambda Y_t) = f_t(X_t, Y_t)$ and thus there exists a unique pricing function g such that $f_t(X_t, Y_t) = g_t\left(\frac{X_t}{Y_t}\right)$ which is the one-dimensional reduction of the two-asset model f. In this case the hedge ratios are given as $\frac{\partial f}{\partial X} = \frac{1}{Y_t}\frac{\partial g}{\partial R}$, $\frac{\partial f}{\partial Y} = -\frac{X_t}{Y_t^2}\frac{\partial g}{\partial R}$ where $R = \frac{X}{Y}$. Remarkably enough the corresponding hedge is then a zero-cost variance dispersion with leg ratio $\beta_0(t) = \left|\frac{\partial f}{\partial Y} / \frac{\partial f}{\partial X}\right| = \frac{X_t}{Y_t} = R_t$.

This general property shows that the pricing and hedging of correlation swaps is strongly interconnected with variance dispersion trading.

PROBLEMS

7.1

Consider a zero-cost vanilla dispersion trade.

(a) Show that β_0 must be comprised between 0 and 1 under penalty of arbitrage.

(b) Derive the proxy $\beta_0 \approx \dfrac{\sigma^*_{\text{Basket}}}{\sum_{i=1}^{n} w_i \sigma^*_i}$ for at-the-money-forward straddles.

7.2

(a) In the Black-Scholes model with zero interest rates, show that the expectation at time 0 of the future dollar gamma of a European option at horizon t is given as:

$$\mathbb{E}\left(\frac{1}{2}\Gamma_t S_t^2\right) = \frac{1}{2}\Gamma_0 S_0^2$$

where Γ_t is the option's gamma at time t and S_t is the underlying asset price at time t.

Hint: Use the Black-Scholes partial differential equation and the Ito-Doeblin theorem to show that $\mathbb{E}_t\left[d\left(\frac{1}{2}\sigma^2\Gamma_t S_t^2\right)\right] = 0$.

(b) Consider a vanilla dispersion trade with leg ratio β. Assume zero rates and dividends and that all realized volatilities are constant. Show that the expectation of the total delta-hedging P&L is then:

$$\Gamma^\$_{0,\text{Basket}}(\sigma^2_{\text{Basket}} - \sigma^{*2}_{\text{Basket}})T - \beta\sum_{i=1}^{n} w_i\Gamma^\$_{0,i}(\sigma^2_i - \sigma^{*2}_i)T$$

7.3

Consider a variance dispersion trade with leg ratio β. Show that if $\beta = \dfrac{\sigma^{\star}_{\text{Basket}}}{\sum_{i=1}^{n} w_i \sigma^{\star}_i}$ the portfolio is initially vega-neutral (i.e., algebraically insensitive to changes in implied volatility).

7.4

Download the market data for the DAX and its 30 constituents from www.wiley.com/go/bossu and calculate the payoffs of:

- A three-month zero-cost at-the-money vanilla dispersion trade:

$$\left| \frac{\text{Index}_T}{\text{Index}_0} - 1 \right| - \widehat{\beta}_0 \sum_{i=1}^{30} w_i \left| \frac{S_T^{(i)}}{S_0^{(i)}} - 1 \right| \quad \text{where} \quad \widehat{\beta}_0 = \frac{\sigma_{\text{Index}}^{\text{ATM}*}}{\sum_{i=1}^{30} w_i \sigma_i^{\text{ATM}*}}$$

- A three-month zero-cost variance dispersion trade

$$\sigma_{\text{Index}}^2 - \beta_0 \sum_{i=1}^{n} w_i \sigma_i^2 \quad \text{where} \quad \beta_0 = \frac{\sigma_{\text{Index}}^{\star 2}}{\sum_{i=1}^{n} w_i \sigma_i^{\star 2}}$$

- A three-month correlation swap:

$$\frac{\sum\limits_{i<j} w_i w_j \rho_{i,j}}{\sum\limits_{i<j} w_i w_j} - K_{\text{correl}}$$

CHAPTER 8

Local Correlation

Local correlation models are a recent cutting-edge development in derivatives modeling and extend the concept of local volatility to multiple assets. Indeed if the volatility of each asset is thought to depend on time and the spot price, then the same idea should probably apply to the correlation coefficient between any two assets. However there are theoretical and practical issues: on the theoretical side the entire correlation matrix must remain positive-definite, which can be challenging; and on the practical side there are very few observable basket option prices to calibrate to. In this chapter we give evidence of non-constant implied correlation and introduce a model that is consistent with this behavior.

8-1 THE IMPLIED CORRELATION SMILE AND ITS CONSEQUENCES

Just as there is an implied volatility smile for options on single stocks, there is also an implied volatility smile for basket options, which is best observed on index options. Figure 8.1 compares the six-month smile on the EuroStoxx 50 index versus the average six-month smile on its constituents. We can see that the slope of the index smile is different from the slope of the constituents' smile, a phenomenon that may only be reproduced by having a different correlation parameter for each moneyness level.

Specifically, for fixed maturity T, we may extract the implied correlation curve by means of the formula:

$$\rho^*(k) = \frac{\sigma_{Basket}^{*2}(k) - \sum_{i=1}^{n} w_i^2 \sigma_i^{*2}(k)}{\left(\sum_{i=1}^{n} w_i \sigma_i^*(k) \right)^2 - \sum_{i=1}^{n} w_i^2 \sigma_i^{*2}(k)} \sim \left[\frac{\sigma_{Basket}^*(k)}{\sum_{i=1}^{n} w_i \sigma_i^*(k)} \right]^2$$

where σ^*'s are implied volatilities, w's are basket weights, and k is the moneyness level.

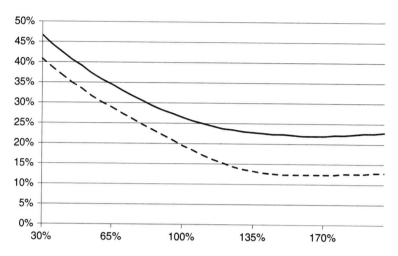

FIGURE 8.1 Six-month smile on the Dow Jones EuroStoxx 50 index versus the average six-month smile on its 50 constituents as of April 30, 2013. *Data source:* OptionMetrics.

Figure 8.2 shows the implied correlation smile obtained on the Dow Jones EuroStoxx 50 index. We can see that the shape is downward sloping, which is consistent with the intuition that when markets go down correlation goes up.

This phenomenon suggests that the constant correlation assumption often used to price basket exotics is not correct, opening the way for yet more sophisticated models. This particularly affects the pricing of worst-of and best-of options, which are very sensitive to the level of input correlation.

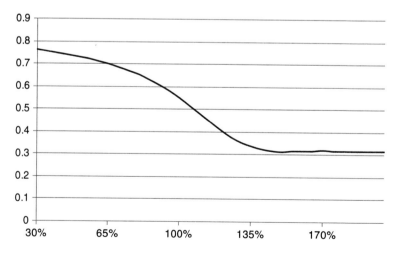

FIGURE 8.2 Six-month implied correlation on the Dow Jones EuroStoxx 50 index as of April 30, 2013.

8-2 LOCAL VOLATILITY WITH LOCAL CORRELATION

A local volatility model with local correlation (LVLC) allows the pairwise correlation coefficients to depend on time and spot prices:

$$
\begin{cases}
dS_t^{(1)} = \mu_1 S_t^{(1)} dt + \sigma_1^{\mathrm{loc}}\left(t, S_t^{(1)}\right) S_t^{(1)} dW_t^{(1)} \\[2mm]
dS_t^{(2)} = \mu_2 S_t^{(2)} dt + \sigma_2^{\mathrm{loc}}\left(t, S_t^{(2)}\right) S_t^{(2)} dW_t^{(2)} \\[2mm]
\quad\vdots \\[2mm]
dS_t^{(n)} = \mu_n S_t^{(n)} dt + \sigma_n^{\mathrm{loc}}\left(t, S_t^{(n)}\right) S_t^{(n)} dW_t^{(n)}
\end{cases}
$$

and

$$
\text{for all } i \neq j: \qquad dW_t^{(i)} dW_t^{(j)} = \rho_{i,j}^{\mathrm{loc}}\left(t, S_t^{(i)}, S_t^{(j)}\right) dt
$$

where $\sigma_i^{\mathrm{loc}}(t, S)$ is the local volatility function for asset $S^{(i)}$ (see Chapter 4) and $\rho_{i,j}^{\mathrm{loc}}(t, S^{(i)}, S^{(j)})$ is a local correlation function for assets $S^{(i)}$ and $S^{(j)}$.

There are many ways to specify the $n(n-1)/2$ local correlation functions $\rho_{i,j}^{\mathrm{loc}}$ and in fact some authors let them depend on the entire vector of spot prices $(S^{(1)}, S^{(2)}, \ldots, S^{(n)})$. The key practical difficulty here is to ensure that the local correlation matrices $R(t, S^{(1)}, \ldots, S^{(n)}) = [\rho_{i,j}^{\mathrm{loc}}(t, S^{(i)}, S^{(j)})]_{1 \leq i,j \leq n}$ are positive-definite at all times and across all spot levels.

It is worth nothing that the arbitrage argument leading to a pricing equation for basket options still holds in the case of LVLC models.

When delta-hedging using an LVLC model, the mismatch between the option payoff and the proceeds of the delta-hedging strategy involves $n(n+1)/2$ terms corresponding to the gammas and cross-gammas. In the two-asset case with zero interest rates the P&L expression is:

$$
\begin{aligned}
\text{P\&L} = {} & \int_0^T \Gamma_1^\$ \left(t, S_t^{(1)}, S_t^{(2)}\right) \left[\left(\frac{dS_t^{(1)}}{S_t^{(1)}}\right)^2 - \left(\sigma_1^{\mathrm{loc}}\left(t, S_t^{(1)}\right)\right)^2 dt \right] \\
& + \int_0^T \Gamma_2^\$ \left(t, S_t^{(1)}, S_t^{(2)}\right) \left[\left(\frac{dS_t^{(2)}}{S_t^{(2)}}\right)^2 - \left(\sigma_2^{\mathrm{loc}}\left(t, S_t^{(2)}\right)\right)^2 dt \right] \\
& + \int_0^T \Gamma_{1,2}^\$ \left(t, S_t^{(1)}, S_t^{(2)}\right) \\
& \quad \times \left[\frac{dS_t^{(1)}}{S_t^{(1)}} \frac{dS_t^{(2)}}{S_t^{(2)}} - \sigma_1^{\mathrm{loc}}\left(t, S_t^{(1)}\right) \sigma_2^{\mathrm{loc}}\left(t, S_t^{(2)}\right) \rho_{1,2}^{\mathrm{loc}}\left(t, S_t^{(1)}, S_t^{(2)}\right) dt \right]
\end{aligned}
$$

where $\Gamma_i^\$ = \frac{1}{2}\frac{\partial^2 f}{\partial S^{(i)2}}S^{(i)2}$ and $\Gamma_{1,2}^\$ = \frac{\partial^2 f}{\partial S^{(1)}S^{(2)}}S^{(1)}S^{(2)}$. We can see that correlation (actually covariance) only appears in the cross-gamma term, and thus the only way to eliminate correlation exposure is by dynamically trading another basket option.

In practice, exotic option traders tend to mitigate their risk by gamma-hedging their exotic position using single-stock listed vanilla options, but they typically do not cross-gamma-hedge with basket options because these are too illiquid and expensive.

FOCUS ON SPREAD OPTION HEDGING

The case of the spread option with payoff $\max\left(0, \frac{S_T^{(1)}}{S_0^{(1)}} - \frac{S_T^{(2)}}{S_0^{(2)}} - k\right)$ is very informative. If correlation is very high and volatilities are similar, the dollar gamma terms tend to cancel each other and we are mostly left with the cross-gamma term:

$$P\&L \approx \int_0^T \Gamma_{1,2}^\$(t, S_t^{(1)}, S_t^{(2)})$$

$$\times \left[\frac{dS_t^{(1)}}{S_t^{(1)}}\frac{dS_t^{(2)}}{S_t^{(2)}} - \sigma_1^{loc}(t, S_t^{(1)})\sigma_2^{loc}(t, S_t^{(2)})\rho_{1,2}^{loc}(t, S_t^{(1)}, S_t^{(2)})dt\right]$$

To make matters worse, the deltas also tend to cancel each other. Thus any traditional hedging strategy (delta- and gamma-hedging) is rather inefficient.

This configuration may be apprehended geometrically: if x and y are two nearly collinear vectors of similar lengths, then $x - y$ is nearly orthogonal, and neither x nor y can efficiently be used to reproduce the spread.

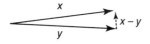

8-3 DYNAMIC LOCAL CORRELATION MODELS

Langnau (2010) and Reghai (2010) both explored a class of LVLC models where local correlations fluctuate between two given "up" and "down" correlation matrices U and D through the convex combination[1]:

$$R(t, \vec{S}) = [\rho_{i,j}^{\text{loc}}\left(t, \vec{S}\right)]_{1 \leq i,j \leq n} = (1 - \alpha(t, \vec{S}))D + \alpha(t, \vec{S})U \qquad (8.1)$$

where $0 \leq \alpha \leq 1$. It is easy to verify that if D and U are positive-definite then so is R.

Langnau shows that if the basket local volatility function $\sigma_{\text{Basket}}^{\text{loc}}(t, B)$ is known, then α is uniquely determined. Specifically, Langnau argues that, subject to certain arbitrage conditions, we must have:

$$\left[\sigma_{\text{Basket}}^{\text{loc}}\left(t, B_t\right)\right]^2 B_t^2 = \sum_{i,j} w_i w_j S_t^{(i)} S_t^{(j)} \sigma_i^{\text{loc}}(t, S_t^{(i)}) \sigma_j^{\text{loc}}(t, S_t^{(j)}) \rho_{i,j}^{\text{loc}}(t, \vec{S})$$

where $B_t = \sum_{i=1}^{n} w_i S_t^{(i)}$ is the basket price. Substituting Equation (8.1) and solving for α we obtain:

$$\alpha(t, \vec{S}) = \frac{\left[\sigma_{\text{Basket}}^{\text{loc}}\left(t, B_t\right)\right]^2 B_t^2 - \text{cov}_D(t, \vec{S})}{\text{cov}_U(t, \vec{S}) - \text{cov}_D(t, \vec{S})}$$

where $\text{cov}_A(t, \vec{S}) = \sum_{1 \leq i,j \leq n} w_i w_j S_t^{(i)} S_t^{(j)} \sigma_i^{\text{loc}}(t, S_t^{(i)}) \sigma_j^{\text{loc}}(t, S_t^{(j)}) a_{ij}$ for any matrix $A = (a_{i,j})$. Note that $\text{cov}_A = x^T A x$ for the vector x with entries $x_i = w_i S_t^{(i)} \sigma_i^{\text{loc}}(t, S_t^{(i)})$.

Langnau's dynamic local correlation model reproduces the index smile very accurately as shown in Figure 8.3 and as such constitutes a significant advance in basket option pricing. In particular, it correctly prices basket variance swaps (without producing a correct hedging strategy).

8-4 LIMITATIONS

The LVLC approach will satisfactorily price a wide range of basket exotics and yield more accurate hedge ratios than the traditional LVCC approach.

---

[1]We slightly redefined α versus Langnau's paper so that $R = D$ for $\alpha = 0$ and $R = U$ for $\alpha = 1$.

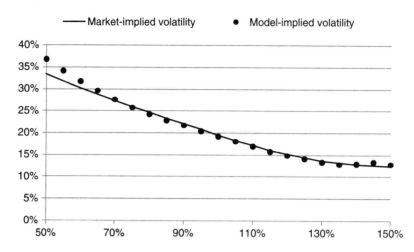

FIGURE 8.3 The dynamic local correlation model reproduces the one-year Dow Jones EuroStoxx 50 index smile as of April 30, 2013, very accurately. *Data source:* OptionMetrics.

However, it will not generate realistic implied volatility and correlation smile dynamics for basket cliquet options, for example, for which a stochastic volatility and correlation model would be required.

Additionally the LVLC approach will not produce a meaningful hedging strategy for new generation payoffs such as correlation swaps.

REFERENCES

Langnau, Alex. 2010. "A Dynamic Model for Correlation." *Risk Magazine* (April): 74–78.

Reghai, Adil. 2010. "Breaking Correlation Breaks." *Risk Magazine* (October): 90–95.

PROBLEMS

8.1 Implied Correlation

Consider a stock index made of n constituent stocks with fixed weights $w_1, \ldots, w_n$. For fixed maturity T, let $a(k)$ denote the implied volatility of the index at moneyness k, and $b(k)$ denote the average implied volatility of the constituent stocks at moneyness k. Show that implied correlation $\frac{a^2(k)}{b^2(k)}$ is constant if and only if the percentage slopes of a and b are equal (i.e., $a'/a = b'/b$).

8.2 Dynamic Local Correlation I

Consider Langnau's dynamic local correlation model with $D = I$ and $U = ee^T$, where I is the identity matrix and e is the vector of 1's. Show that

$$\alpha = \frac{\left(\sigma_{Basket}^{loc}\right)^2 - \sum_{i=1}^{n} x_i^2 \sigma_i^{loc2}}{\left(\sum_{i=1}^{n} x_i \sigma_i^{loc}\right)^2 - \sum_{i=1}^{n} x_i^2 \sigma_i^{loc2}}$$ for a particular choice of nonnegative weights

x summing to 1, and then argue that $\alpha = \rho(x)$ where $\rho(x)$ is defined in Equation (6.1).

8.3 Dynamic Local Correlation II

This is a continuation of Problem 8.2.
Assume for ease of implementation that:

- The Dow Jones EuroStoxx 50 index is made of 50 equally weighted constituent stocks
- Interest and dividend rates are zero
- All implied volatility surfaces have the following parametric form

$$\sigma^*(k, T) = \sqrt{\frac{\theta}{2} \left[1 + \rho\varphi_\lambda(\theta) \ln k + \sqrt{(\varphi_\lambda(\theta) \ln k + \rho)^2 + 1 - \rho^2} \right]}$$

where $k = K/S$ is moneyness, $\theta > 0$, $-1 \le \rho \le 1$, $\lambda \ge 0.5$ are time-independent parameters and:

$$\varphi_\lambda(\theta) = \frac{1}{\lambda\theta} \left(1 - \frac{1 - e^{-\lambda\theta}}{\lambda\theta} \right)$$

Download the parameters for the index and its constituents from www .wiley.com/go/bossu and then implement Langnau's dynamic local correlation model with $D = I$ and $U = ee^T$ to price one-year arbitrary basket payoffs using 252 time steps. Reproduce Figure 8.3 and then verify that the price of a 50% worst-of call on the 50 constituents is approximately 11.3%.

Hint: You will need to compute time-dependent local volatilities using Equation (4.2).

CHAPTER 9

Stochastic Correlation

Stochastic correlation models may provide a more realistic approach to the pricing and hedging of certain types of exotic derivatives, such as worst-of and best-of options and correlation swaps and correlation options. In this chapter, we review various types of stochastic correlation models and propose a framework for the pricing of realized correlation derivatives that is consistent with variance swap markets.

9-1 STOCHASTIC SINGLE CORRELATION

Consider the following general model framework for two assets $S^{(1)}$ and $S^{(2)}$:

$$\begin{cases} dS_t^{(1)}/S_t^{(1)} = \mu_1(t,\dots)dt + \sigma_1(t,\dots)dW_t^{(1)} \\ dS_t^{(2)}/S_t^{(2)} = \mu_2(t,\dots)dt + \sigma_2(t,\dots)dW_t^{(2)} \\ (dW_t^{(1)})(dW_t^{(2)}) = \rho(t,\dots)dt \end{cases}$$

where μ's are instant drift coefficients, σ's are instant volatility coefficients, and ρ is the instant correlation coefficient between the driving Brownian motions W's. Here all the coefficients may be stochastic, and we focus on ρ.

There are some simple ways to make ρ stochastic and comprised between -1 and 1; for example, take $\rho_t = \sin(\alpha + \beta Z_t)$ where Z is an independent Brownian motion. The dynamics of $d\rho_t$ may then be found by means of the Ito-Doeblin theorem. One issue with this approach is that the parameters may not be very intuitive.

A better approach is to specify diffusion dynamics for ρ and examine the Feller conditions at bounds -1 and 1 (see Section 2-4.2.2). A popular process here is the affine Jacobi process, also known as a Fischer-Wright

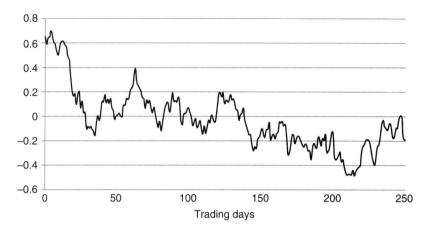

FIGURE 9.1 Sample path of an affine Jacobi process with parameters $\rho_0 = 0.65$, $\bar{\rho} = -0.1, \kappa = 10.6, \alpha = 1$.

process, which is very similar to Heston's stochastic volatility process (see Section 2-4.2.2):

$$d\rho_t = \kappa(\bar{\rho} - \rho_t)dt + \alpha\sqrt{1 - \rho_t^2}dZ_t$$

where $\bar{\rho}$ is the long-term mean, κ is the mean reversion speed, and α is the volatility of instant correlation. The Feller condition is then $\frac{\alpha^2}{\kappa} - 1 < \bar{\rho} < 1 - \frac{\alpha^2}{\kappa}$. A technical analysis of this type of process can be found in van Emmerich (2006).

Figure 9.1 shows the path obtained for an affine Jacobi process with parameters $\rho_0 = 0.65, \bar{\rho} = -0.1, \kappa = 10.6, \alpha = 1$. Observe how all values are comprised between -1 and 1.

9-2 STOCHASTIC AVERAGE CORRELATION

We now shift our focus to average correlation measures $\rho(x) = \dfrac{\sum\limits_{i<j} x_i x_j \rho_{i,j}}{\sum\limits_{i<j} x_i x_j}$ as introduced in Section 6-3. Because the correlation matrix $R = (\rho_{i,j})_{1 \leq i,j \leq n}$ must be positive-definite at all times we cannot naively extend the single correlation case with, for instance, $n(n-1)/2$ affine Jacobi processes and take their average. Note that as a consequence of positive-definiteness $\rho(x)$ is actually comprised between 0 and 1 for large n.

Before we go into further detail we must distinguish between nontradable correlation, such as rolling historical or implied correlations, and tradable correlation, such as the historical correlation observed over a fixed time period $[0, T]$:

- Nontradable average correlation can be modeled quite freely, using, for example, a standard Jacobi process between 0 and 1 or econometric processes such as Constant and Dynamic Conditional Correlation models (see, e.g., Engle (2009)).
- Tradable average correlation requires special consideration to be consistent with other related securities such as variance swaps.

The rest of this section is devoted to the study of tradable average correlation.

9-2.1 Tradable Average Correlation

Consider $\widehat{\rho} = \frac{\sigma_{Basket}^2}{\sum_{i=1}^n w_i \sigma_i^2}$ which was introduced in Section 7-1.2 and is related

to the proxy formula $\widehat{\rho} = \left(\frac{\sigma_{Basket}}{\sum_{i=1}^n w_i \sigma_i} \right)^2$ introduced in Section 6-3.1. Because

$\widehat{\rho}$ is the ratio of two tradable assets—namely, basket variance and average constituent variance—we can derive its dynamics from those of the two tradable assets. For example, suppose we have:

$$\begin{cases} dX_t/X_t = f_t\left(X_t, Y_t\right) dW_t \\ dY_t/Y_t = g_t(X_t, Y_t)dZ_t \\ (dW_t)(dZ_t) = h_t(X_t, Y_t)dt \end{cases}$$

where X_t is the price of basket variance at time t, $Y_t \geq X_t$ is the price of average constituent variance at time t, and the driving Brownian motions W, Z are taken under the forward-neutral measure.

Using the Ito-Doeblin theorem the resulting dynamics for $\widehat{\rho} = \frac{X}{Y}$ are then:

$$d\widehat{\rho}_t/\widehat{\rho}_t = (g_t^2 - f_t g_t h_t)dt + \sqrt{f_t^2 - 2f_t g_t h_t + g_t^2}dB_t \qquad (9.1)$$

where B is another standard Brownian motion constructed from W and Z.

Note that, as the ratio of two prices, $\widehat{\rho}_t$ is **not** the price of correlation at time t, which is why the drift coefficient in Equation (9.1) is nonzero under the forward-neutral measure:

$$\widehat{\rho}_t = \frac{X_t}{Y_t} = \frac{\mathbb{E}_t(X_T)}{\mathbb{E}_t(Y_T)} \neq \mathbb{E}_t\left(\frac{X_T}{Y_T}\right) = \mathbb{E}_t(\widehat{\rho}_T)$$

Because $\hat{\rho}$ is invariant when multiplying X and Y by the same scalar λ, we may further focus on one-dimensional reductions of the model (see Section 7-2.3) and assume that f, g, h are functions of X/Y:

$$\begin{cases} dX_t/X_t = f_t\left(\dfrac{X_t}{Y_t}\right)dW_t \\[3mm] dY_t/Y_t = g_t\left(\dfrac{X_t}{Y_t}\right)dZ_t \\[3mm] (dW_t)(dZ_t) = h_t\left(\dfrac{X_t}{Y_t}\right)dt \end{cases}$$

In this case Equation (9.1) becomes one-dimensional; that is, the drift and volatility coefficients depend only on time and $\hat{\rho}_t$. This makes the following Feller analysis considerably easier.

Omitting the time subscript for ease of exposition and using x to denote the state variable we may rewrite Equation (9.1) as:

$$dx = \left[g^2(x) - f(x)g(x)h(x)\right]x\,dt + x\sqrt{f^2(x) - 2f(x)g(x)h(x) + g^2(x)}\,dB \tag{9.2}$$

The Feller conditions at bounds 0 and 1 are then:

$$\begin{cases} \displaystyle\lim_{x\downarrow 0}\int_x^{x_0} s(y)\,dy = \infty \\[4mm] \displaystyle\lim_{x\uparrow 1}\int_{x_0}^{x} s(y)\,dy = \infty \\[4mm] s(y) = \exp\left(-\displaystyle\int_{y_0}^{y}\dfrac{2\left[g^2(u) - f(u)g(u)h(u)\right]}{u[f^2(u) - 2f(u)g(u)h(u) + g^2(u)]}\,du\right) \end{cases}$$

Dividing both the numerator and denominator by $g^2(u)$, the integrand in $s(y)$ may be rewritten as $\frac{1}{u}\left[1 + \frac{1-p^2(u)}{p^2(u)-2p(u)h(u)+1}\right]$ with $p(u) = \frac{f(u)}{g(u)}$. Furthermore,

- As $x \to 0$ a sufficient condition is that $\lim_0 \frac{1-p^2}{p^2-2ph+1} = \ell \geq 0$ in which case we have $s(y) \approx \exp\left(-\int_{y_0}^{y}\frac{1+\ell}{u}du\right) = \left(\frac{y_0}{y}\right)^{1+\ell}$ for y_0 and y close to 0, and thus $\lim_{x\downarrow 0}\int_x^{x_0} s(y)dy = \infty$. A formal proof of sufficiency is proposed in Appendix 9.A.

- As $x \to 1$ a necessary condition is that $s(y) \to \infty$, which in turn implies that $\frac{1-p^2}{p^2-2ph+1}$ diverges (see Appendix 9.B for a formal proof). An analysis of this quantity over the domain $p \geq 0$ and $|h| \leq 1$ reveals that the only singularity is at $(1, 1)$. Thus, as a corollary we have the weak necessary condition $f(u) \sim g(u)$ and $h(u) \rightarrow 1$ as $u \rightarrow 1$. This configuration intuitively makes sense: if average correlation is close to 1, there is almost no diversification effect, and basket variance and average constituent variance become almost identical.

Additionally, we want $f \geq g$ because basket variance is more volatile than average constituent variance, which unfortunately makes the sufficient condition stated above ineffective, since $p \geq 1$. We must keep all these properties in mind when researching suitable functions f, g, and h.

9-2.2 The B-O Model

The following model, which we call the B-O model (for beta-omega), is a further step towards a suitable stochastic average correlation model:

$$\begin{cases} dX_t/X_t = 2\frac{T-t}{T}\left[\omega + \beta\left(1 - \frac{X_t}{Y_t}\right)\right]dW_t \\ dY_t/Y_t = 2\omega\frac{T-t}{T}dZ_t \\ (dW_t)(dZ_t) = \left[\frac{X_t}{Y_t} + \frac{\omega}{\omega+\beta}\left(1 - \frac{X_t}{Y_t}\right)\right]dt \end{cases} \tag{9.3}$$

where ω is the instant volatility of constituent volatility and β is the "additional" volatility of basket volatility.[1] The corresponding dynamics for the average correlation $\widehat{\rho} \equiv x$ are then given by Equation (9.2) using the functions:

$$\begin{cases} f_t(x) = 2\frac{T-t}{T}[\omega + \beta(1 - x)] \\ g_t(x) = 2\omega\frac{T-t}{T} \\ h_t(x) = x + \frac{\omega}{\omega+\beta}(1 - x) \end{cases}$$

Unfortunately, both lower and upper bounds [0,1] turn out to be attracting in the B-O model, making it unsuitable for extreme starting values ρ_0 and long-term horizons T. However, empirical simulations exhibit plausible paths. Further research is needed here.

Figure 9.2 shows 10 sample paths obtained with parameters $\omega = 70\%$, $\beta = 40\%$ and $\widehat{\rho}_0 = 0.5$. Remarkably enough, using Monte Carlo simulations the price of correlation $\mathbb{E}(\widehat{\rho}_T)$ in this model appears to be close to the initial value $\widehat{\rho}_0 = \frac{X_0}{Y_0} = \frac{\sigma^{*2}_{\text{Basket}}}{\sum_{i=1}^{n} w_i \sigma^{*2}_i}$, also known as variance-implied correlation. This suggests that the fair strike of a correlation swap on $\widehat{\rho}_T$ should

---

[1]Note that $dX_t/X_t = 2(\omega + \beta)\frac{T-t}{T}dW_t$ when $\widehat{\rho}_t = X_t/Y_t$ is equal to 0, and that $dX_t/X_t = 2\omega\frac{T-t}{T}dW_t$ when $\widehat{\rho}_t$ is equal to 1.

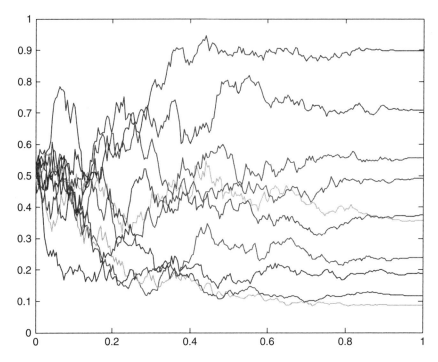

FIGURE 9.2 Ten sample paths using the B-O model with parameters $\omega = 70\%$, $\beta = 40\%$, and $\widehat{\rho}_0 = 0.5$.

be close to $\widehat{\rho}_0$, and by extension a similar result should apply to standard correlation swaps.

9-3 STOCHASTIC CORRELATION MATRIX

A yet more ambitious endeavor is to devise a model for the evolution of the entire correlation matrix $R_t = (\rho_{i,j}(t))_{1 \leq i,j \leq n}$ through time. As pointed out earlier, the difficulty here is to ensure that R_t is positive-definite at all times.

It is worth emphasizing that, when correlations are tradable, we should also ensure that the induced dynamics of average correlation $\widehat{\rho}_t$ be consistent with variance swaps under the forward-neutral measure.

As already pointed out in Section 6-2, equity correlation matrices have structure—namely, there is typically one large eigenvalue dominating all others, and the associated eigenvector corresponds to an all-stock portfolio. As such an equity correlation matrix cannot be viewed as any kind of random matrix.

Here we need to be more specific about the meaning of a (symmetric) random matrix. This concept was first introduced by Wishart (1928) in the form $M = XX^T$ where X is an $n \times n$ matrix of independent and identically distributed random variables; the special case where X is Gaussian deserves particular attention since it tends to the identity matrix as $n \to \infty$. Another approach is Wigner's, whereby $M = \frac{1}{2}(X + X^T)$; a remarkable property is that the empirical distribution of ordered eigenvalues then follows the semi-circle law:

$$\frac{1}{n} \#\{i : \lambda_i \leq \lambda\} \xrightarrow[n \to \infty]{} \frac{1}{2\pi} \int_{-2}^{\lambda} \sqrt{4 - x^2} dx \quad (|\lambda| \leq 2)$$

9-3.1 Spectral Decomposition and the Common Factor Model

The empirical analysis of equity correlation matrices suggests that they may be viewed as the sum of a (truly) random matrix and an orthogonal projector onto the maximal eigenvector. Following the spectral theorem we may indeed write:

$$R = \left(\sum_{i=1}^{n-1} \lambda_i v_i v_i^T \right) + \lambda_n v_n v_n^T$$

where $(v_1, \ldots, v_n)$ is an orthonormal basis of eigenvectors with eigenvalues $\lambda_1 \leq \cdots \leq \lambda_n$. The residual matrix $\sum_{i=1}^{n-1} \lambda_i v_i v_i^T = R - \lambda_n v_n v_n^T$ may then be approximated by a Wishart-type matrix.

For large n we could ignore $\sum_{i=1}^{n-1} \lambda_i v_i v_i^T$ altogether and write:

$$R \approx \widehat{R} = (I - \lambda_n D) + \lambda_n v_n v_n^T = \begin{pmatrix} 1 & \lambda_n a_1 a_2 & \cdots & \lambda_n a_1 a_n \\ \lambda_n a_2 a_1 & 1 & & \lambda_n a_2 a_n \\ \vdots & & \ddots & \vdots \\ \lambda_n a_n a_1 & \lambda_n a_n a_2 & \cdots & 1 \end{pmatrix}$$

where $a_1, \ldots, a_n$ are the entries of the maximal eigenvector v_n and $D = diag(a_1^2, \ldots, a_n^2)$. Note that $\widehat{R}$ has different eigenelements from R; however, λ_n is related to average correlation because $\rho(\widehat{R}; v_n) = \dfrac{v_n^T \widehat{R} v_n - 1}{(v_n^T e)^2 - 1} = \dfrac{\lambda_n}{n} \dfrac{1 - \sum_{i=1}^{n} a_i^4}{\frac{1}{n}(v_n^T e)^2 - \frac{1}{n}} \sim \dfrac{\lambda_n / n}{\cos^2(\widehat{v_n, e})}$ as $n \to \infty$.

This approach corroborates Boortz's Common Factor Model (2008) whereby:

$$R_t = \begin{pmatrix} 1 & \xi_{t,1}\xi_{t,2} & \cdots & \xi_{t,1}\xi_{t,n} \\ \xi_{t,2}\xi_{t,1} & 1 & & \xi_{t,2}\xi_{t,n} \\ \vdots & & \ddots & \vdots \\ \xi_{t,n}\xi_{t,1} & \xi_{t,n}\xi_{t,2} & \cdots & 1 \end{pmatrix}$$

where $(\xi_{t,1}, \dots, \xi_{t,n})$ is a vector of correlated stochastic processes in $(-1, 1)$, such as affine Jacobi processes. One issue with the Common Factor Model is that the (equally weighted) average realized correlation has a risk-neutral drift, which has no particular reason to fit in the framework of Section 9-2.1. In other words the Common Factor Model does not appear to be consistent with variance swap markets.

9-3.2 The $n \times n$ Fischer-Wright Model

Recent work by Ahdida and Alfonsi (2012) alternatively proposes the following stochastic process for the correlation matrix R_t, which is a generalization of the Jacobi process:

$$dR_t = \left[\kappa \left(\overline{R} - R_t \right) + (\overline{R} - R_t)\kappa \right] dt$$

$$+ \sum_{i=1}^{n} \alpha_i \left(\sqrt{R_t - R_t E_{i,i} R_t} \, dW_t E_{i,i} + E_{i,i} dW_t^T \sqrt{R_t - R_t E_{i,i} R_t} \right)$$

where the matrix $\overline{R}$ is the long-term correlation mean, $\kappa = diag(\kappa_1, \dots, \kappa_n)$ is a diagonal matrix of mean-reversion speeds, $\alpha = diag(\alpha_1, \dots, \alpha_n)$ is a diagonal matrix of volatility coefficients, $E_{i,i} = diag(0, \dots, 0, 1, 0, \dots, 0)$ is the diagonal matrix with coefficient 1 at position (i,i) and 0 elsewhere, $\sqrt{H}$ denotes the unique square root of a positive-semidefinite matrix H, and (W_t) is an $n \times n$ matrix of independent standard Brownian motions.

Subject to the condition $\kappa \overline{R} + \overline{R} \kappa - (n-2)\alpha^2$ being positive-semidefinite, the Ahdida-Alfonsi process is guaranteed to remain a valid correlation matrix through time; however, a corrected Euler scheme is required for simulation.

Unfortunately, Ahdida and Alfonsi have not studied the eigenelements of their respective correlation matrix processes. and it is difficult to tell how realistic their model is within the realm of equity correlation matrices. In particular, there is no guarantee that the induced dynamics of average correlation can be made consistent with realistic dynamics of basket variance and average constituent variance in the fashion described early in the chapter. Further research is thus needed.

REFERENCES

Ahdida, Abdelkoddousse, and Aurélien Alfonsi. 2012. "A Mean-Reverting SDE on Correlation Matrices." arXiv:1108.5264.

Boortz, C. Kaya. 2008. "Modelling Correlation Risk." Diplomarbeit preprint, Institut für Mathematik, Technische Universität Berlin & Quantitative Products Laboratory, Deutsche Bank AG.

Engle, Robert. 2009. *Anticipating Correlations: A New Paradigm for Risk Management*. Princeton, NJ: Princeton University Press.

van Emmerich, Cathrin. 2006. "Modelling Correlation as a Stochastic Process." Bergische Universität Wuppertal. Preprint.

Wishart, John. 1928. "The Generalised Product Moment Distribution in Samples from a Normal Multivariate Population." *Biometrika* 20A (1–2): 32–52.

PROBLEMS

9.1

Consider a stock S, which does not pay dividends, with dollar price $S^\$$, and let X be the exchange rate of one dollar into euros. Assume that $S^\$$ and X both follow geometric Brownian motions under the dollar risk-neutral measure with joint dynamics:

$$\begin{cases} dS_t^\$ / S_t^\$ = r_\$ dt + \sigma dW_t \\ dX_t / X_t = v dt + \eta dZ_t \end{cases}$$

where $r_\$$ is the constant dollar interest rate, σ, v and η are free constant parameters, and W, Z are standard Brownian motions with stochastic correlation $(dW_t)(dZ_t) \equiv \tilde{\rho}_t dt$.

(a) Show that the forward price of S quanto euro for maturity T is $S_0^\$ \mathbb{E}\left[\exp\left(r_\$ T - \sigma\eta \int_0^T \tilde{\rho}_t dt\right)\right]$.

(b) Assume that $S_0^\$ = \$100$, $r_\$ = 0$, $\sigma = 25\%$, $\eta = 10\%$, $d\rho_t = \kappa(\bar{\rho} - \rho_t)dt + \alpha\sqrt{1 - \rho_t^2}dB_t$ with $\rho_0 = -0.65$, $\bar{\rho} = -0.2$, $\kappa = 10.6$, $\alpha = 1$. Compute the one-year forward price of S quanto euro using Monte Carlo simulations over 252 trading days. *Answer: €100.60*

9.2

Consider the model for stochastic average correlation:

$$d\widehat{\rho}_t/\widehat{\rho}_t = \omega^2(1 - \widehat{\rho}_t)dt + \omega\frac{1 - \widehat{\rho}_t}{\sqrt{1 - \widehat{\rho}_t/2}}dB_t$$

(a) Verify that the process remains within $(0,1)$ and that the lower bound is non-attracting.

(b) Define $h(x) = \sqrt{x(2-x)}$. Find $f(x)$, $g(x)$ such that $\widehat{\rho} \equiv x$ satisfies Equation (9.2). *Hint: Show that* $\frac{1-ph}{p^2-2ph+1} = \frac{1-x/2}{1-x}$ *where* $p = f/g$ *and solve for p.*

(c) Do you think that this model is suitable?

APPENDIX 9.A: SUFFICIENT CONDITION FOR LOWER BOUND UNATTAINABILITY

Following the notations of Section 9-2.1, suppose that $\lim\limits_{0}\frac{1-p^2}{p^2-2ph+1} = \ell \geq 0$. By the definition of a limit this means that for arbitrary $\varepsilon > 0$ there exists an $\alpha > 0$ such that:

$$\text{for all } 0 \leq u \leq \alpha, \frac{1 - p^2(u)}{p^2(u) - 2p(u)h(u) + 1} \leq \ell + \varepsilon$$

Thus, for all $0 < u \leq \alpha$, $-\frac{1}{u}\left[1 + \frac{1-p^2(u)}{p^2(u)-2p(u)h(u)+1}\right] \geq -\frac{1+\ell+\varepsilon}{u}$. By integration over $[y_0, y] \subset [0, \alpha]$ we get:

$$-\int_{y_0}^{y}\frac{du}{u}\left[1 + \frac{1 - p^2(u)}{p^2(u) - 2p(u)h(u) + 1}\right] \geq -\int_{y_0}^{y}\frac{1+\ell+\varepsilon}{u}du$$

$$= -(1 + \ell + \varepsilon)\ln\frac{y}{y_0}.$$

Taking exponentials:

$$s(y) \geq \left(\frac{y_0}{y}\right)^{1+\ell+\varepsilon}$$

and thus $\lim\limits_{x\downarrow 0}\int_{x}^{x_0}s(y)dy = \infty$ since $\int_{0}^{x_0}\frac{dy}{y^{1+\beta}}$ diverges for any $\beta \geq 0$.

APPENDIX 9.B: NECESSARY CONDITION FOR UPPER BOUND UNATTAINABILITY

Suppose that $\frac{1-p^2}{p^2-2ph+1}$ converges to a finite limit ℓ. By the definition of a limit this means that for arbitrary $\varepsilon > 0$ there exists an $\alpha < 1$ such that:

$$\text{for all } \alpha \le u \le 1, \ell - \varepsilon \le \frac{1 - p^2(u)}{p^2(u) - 2p(u)h(u) + 1} \le \ell + \varepsilon$$

Thus, for all $\alpha \le u \le 1$, $\frac{1+\ell-\varepsilon}{u} \le \frac{1}{u}\left[1 + \frac{1-p^2(u)}{p^2(u)-2p(u)h(u)+1}\right] \le \frac{1+\ell+\varepsilon}{u}$. By integration over $[y_0, y] \subset [\alpha, 1]$ we get:

$$(1 + \ell - \varepsilon) \ln \frac{y}{y_0} \le \int_{y_0}^{y} \frac{du}{u}\left[1 + \frac{1 - p^2(u)}{p^2(u) - 2p(u)h(u) + 1}\right] \le (1 + \ell + \varepsilon) \ln \frac{y}{y_0}$$

Taking exponentials:

$$\left(\frac{y_0}{y}\right)^{1+\ell+\varepsilon} \le s(y) \le \left(\frac{y_0}{y}\right)^{1+\ell-\varepsilon}$$

and thus $\lim_{x\uparrow 1} \int_{x_0}^{x} s(y)dy$ is finite since $\int_{x_0}^{1} \frac{dy}{y^\beta}$ converges for any β, thereby contradicting the requirement that $\lim_{x\uparrow 1} \int_{x_0}^{x} s(y)dy = \infty$.

Probability Review

A-1 STANDARD PROBABILITY THEORY

A-1.1 Probability Space

A probability space $(\Omega, \mathcal{A}, \mathbb{P})$ is the provision of:

- A set of all possible outcomes $\omega \in \Omega$, sometimes called states of Nature
- A σ-algebra, that is, a set of measurable events $A \in \mathcal{A}$, which (1) contains $\emptyset$, (2) is stable by complementation ($\overline{A} \in \mathcal{A}$) and (3) is stable by countable unions ($\cup_{i \in \mathbb{N}} A_i \in \mathcal{A}$)
- A probability measure $\mathbb{P}: \mathcal{A} \to [0, 1]$, which (1) satisfies $\mathbb{P}(\Omega) = 1$ and (2) is countably additive ($\mathbb{P}(\bigsqcup_i A_i) = \sum_i \mathbb{P}(A_i)$ where $\bigsqcup$ denotes disjoint union)

A-1.2 Filtered Probability Space

A filtered probability space $(\Omega, \mathcal{A}, (\mathcal{F}_t), \mathbb{P})$ is a probability space equipped with a filtration $(\mathcal{F}_t)$, which is an increasing sequence of σ-algebras (for any $t \leq t': \mathcal{F}_t \subseteq \mathcal{F}_{t'} \subseteq \mathcal{A}$). Informally the filtration represents "information" garnered through time.

A-1.3 Independence

Two events $(A, B) \in \mathcal{A}^2$ are said to be independent whenever their joint probability is the product of individual probabilities:

$$\mathbb{P}(A \cap B) = \mathbb{P}(A) \times \mathbb{P}(B)$$

A-2 RANDOM VARIABLES, DISTRIBUTION, AND INDEPENDENCE

A-2.1 Random Variables

A random variable is a function $X: \Omega \rightarrow \mathbb{R}$ mapping every outcome with a real number, such that the event $\{X \leq x\} \in \mathcal{A}$ for all $x \in \mathbb{R}$. The notation $X \in \mathcal{A}$ is often used to indicate that X satisfies the requirements for a random variable with respect to the σ-algebra $\mathcal{A}$.

The cumulative distribution function of X is then $F_X(x) = \mathbb{P}(X \leq x)$, which is always defined. In most practical applications the probability mass function $\mathbb{P}(X = x)$ or density function $f_X = \frac{\partial F_X}{\partial x}$ (often denoted $\mathbb{P}(X = x)$ as well) contains all the useful information about X.

The mathematical expectation of X, if it exists, is then:

- In general: $\mathbb{E}(X) = \int_\Omega X(\omega)\mathbb{P}(d\omega)$;
- For clearly discrete random variables: $\mathbb{E}(X) = \sum\limits_{x \in X\langle\Omega\rangle} x\mathbb{P}(X = x)$;
- For random variables with density f_X: $\mathbb{E}(X) = \int_{-\infty}^{+\infty} xf_X(x)dx$.

The law of the unconscious statistician states that if X has density f_X the expectation of an arbitrary function $g(X)$ is given by the inner product of f_X and g:

$$\mathbb{E}(g(X)) = \int_{-\infty}^{+\infty} g(x)f_X(x)dx$$

if it exists.

The variance of X, if it exists, is defined as $\mathbb{V}(X) = \mathbb{E}([X - \mathbb{E}(X)]^2) = \mathbb{E}(X^2) - [\mathbb{E}(X)]^2$, and its standard deviation as $\sigma(X) = \sqrt{\mathbb{V}(X)}$.

A-2.2 Joint Distribution and Independence

Given n random variables $X_1, \ldots, X_n$, their joint cumulative distribution function is:

$$F_{(X_1, \ldots, X_n)}(x_1, \ldots, x_n) = \mathbb{P}(\{X_1 \leq x_1\} \cap \cdots \cap \{X_n \leq x_n\})$$

and each individual cumulative distribution function $F_{X_i}(x_i) = \mathbb{P}(X_i \leq x_i)$ is then called "marginal."

The n random variables are said to be independent whenever the joint cumulative distribution function of any subset is equal to the product of the marginal cumulative distribution functions:

For all $\{i_1, \ldots, i_k\} \subseteq \{1, \ldots, n\}$: $F_{(X_{i_1}, \ldots X_{i_k})} = F_{X_{i_1}} \times \cdots \times F_{X_{i_k}}$

The covariance between two random variables X, Y is given as:

$$\text{Cov}(X, Y) = \mathbb{E}(XY) - \mathbb{E}(X)\mathbb{E}(Y)$$

and their correlation coefficient is defined as: $\rho(X, Y) = \frac{\text{Cov}(X,Y)}{\sigma(X)\sigma(Y)} \in [-1,1]$. If X, Y are independent, then their covariance and correlation is zero but the converse is not true. If $\rho = \pm 1$ then $\mathbb{P}(Y = \pm aX + b) = 1$.

The variance of the sum of n random variables $X_1, \ldots, X_n$ is:

$$\mathbb{V}\left(\sum_{i=1}^{n} X_i\right) = \sum_{i=1}^{n} \mathbb{V}(X_i) + 2\sum_{i<j} \text{Cov}(X_i, X_j)$$

If X, Y are independent with densities f_X, f_Y, the density of their sum $X + Y$ is given by the convolution of marginal densities:

$$f_{X+Y} = f_X * f_Y \colon z \mapsto \int_{-\infty}^{+\infty} f_X(x)f_Y(z-x)dx$$

A-3   CONDITIONING

Conditioning is a method to recalculate probabilities using known information. For example, at the French roulette the initial Ω is $\{0, 1, \ldots, 36\}$ but after the ball falls into a colored pocket, we can eliminate several possibilities even as the wheel is still spinning.

The conditional probability of an event A given B is defined as:

$$\mathbb{P}(A|B) = \frac{\mathbb{P}(A \cap B)}{\mathbb{P}(B)}$$

Note that $\mathbb{P}(A|B) = \mathbb{P}(A)$ if A, B are independent.

This straightforwardly leads to the conditional expectation of a random variable X given an event B:

$$\mathbb{E}(X|B) = \int_{\Omega} X(\omega)\mathbb{P}(d\omega|B)$$

Generally, the conditional expectation of X given a σ-algebra $\mathcal{F} \subseteq \mathcal{A}$ can be defined as the random variable $Y \in \mathcal{F}$ such that:

$$\text{For all } A \in \mathcal{F} \colon \int_A X(\omega)\mathbb{P}(d\omega) = \int_A Y(\omega)\mathbb{P}(d\omega)$$

or equivalently: $\mathbb{E}(X1_A) = \mathbb{E}(Y1_A)$. $Y = \mathbb{E}(X|\mathcal{F})$ can be shown to exist and to be unique with probability 1.

The conditional expectation operator shares the usual properties of unconditional expectation (linearity; if $X \geq Y$ then $\mathbb{E}(X|\mathcal{F}) \geq \mathbb{E}(Y|\mathcal{F})$; Jensen's inequality; etc.) and also has the following specific properties:

- If $X \in \mathcal{F}$ then $\mathbb{E}(X|\mathcal{F}) = X$
- If $X \in \mathcal{F}$ and Y is arbitrary then $\mathbb{E}(XY|\mathcal{F}) = X\mathbb{E}(Y|\mathcal{F})$
- Iterated expectations: if $\mathcal{F}_1 \subseteq \mathcal{F}_2$ are σ-algebras then $\mathbb{E}(X|\mathcal{F}_1) = \mathbb{E}(\mathbb{E}(X|\mathcal{F}_2)|\mathcal{F}_1)$. In particular $\mathbb{E}(X) = \mathbb{E}(\mathbb{E}(X|\mathcal{F}))$

A-4   RANDOM PROCESSES AND STOCHASTIC CALCULUS

A random process, or stochastic process, is a sequence (X_t) of random variables. When $X_t \in \mathcal{F}_t$ for all t the process is said to be $(\mathcal{F}_t)$-adapted.

The process (X_t) is called a martingale whenever for all $t < t'$: $X_t = \mathbb{E}(X_{t'}|\mathcal{F}_t)$.

The process (X_t) is said to be predictable whenever for all t: $X_t \in \mathcal{F}_{t-}$ (X_t is knowable prior to t).

The path of a process (X_t) in a given outcome ω is the function $t \mapsto X_t(\omega)$.

A standard Brownian motion or Wiener process (W_t) is a stochastic process with continuous paths that satisfies:

- $W_0 = 0$
- For all $t < t'$ the increment $W_{t'} - W_t$ follows a normal distribution with zero mean and standard deviation $\sqrt{t' - t}$
- Any finite set of nonoverlapping increments $W_{t_2} - W_{t_1}, W_{t_4} - W_{t_3}, \ldots$ is independent.

An Ito process (X_t) is defined by the stochastic differential equation:

$$dX_t = a_t dt + b_t dW_t$$

where W is a standard Brownian motion, (a_t) is a predictable and integrable process, and (b_t) is a predictable and square-integrable process.

The Ito-Doeblin theorem states that a C^2 function $(f(X_t))$ of an Ito process is also an Ito process with stochastic differential equation:

$$df(X_t) = f'(X_t)dX_t + \frac{1}{2}f''(X_t)b_t^2 dt$$

Linear Algebra Review

B-1 EUCLIDEAN SPACES

B-1.1 Inner Product and the Norm

A Euclidean space E is a finite-dimensional vector space for which an inner product $\langle \cdot, \cdot \rangle$ is defined. The inner product, sometimes called dot product and denoted $x \cdot y$, must satisfy the following three axioms:

1. Symmetry: $\langle x, y \rangle = \langle y, x \rangle$
2. Bilinearity: $\langle \lambda x + y, z \rangle = \lambda \langle x, z \rangle + \langle y, z \rangle$ for any $\lambda \in \mathbb{R}$
3. Positive-definiteness: $\langle x, x \rangle \geq 0$ and $\langle x, x \rangle = 0$ if and only if $x = 0$

For example:

- $E = \mathbb{R}^n$ with the canonical dot product $x \cdot y = \sum_{i=1}^{n} x_i y_i = y^T x$
- The space of continuous functions over the interval $[a, b]$ with the inner product:

$$\langle f, g \rangle = \int_a^b f(x)g(x)dx$$

The inner product induces a distance or norm $\|x\| = \sqrt{\langle x, x \rangle}$ with the following standard properties:

- Positive scalability: $\|\lambda x\| = |\lambda| \|x\|$ for any $\lambda \in \mathbb{R}$
- Triangle inequality: $\|x + y\| \leq \|x\| + \|y\|$

B-1.2 Cauchy-Schwarz Inequality and Angles

The Cauchy-Schwarz inequality is one of the most important inequalities in all of mathematics and states that:

$$|\langle x, y \rangle| \leq \|x\| \|y\|$$

which allows us to define the absolute angle in $[0, \pi]$ between x and y as:

$$\widehat{(x, y)} = \arccos \frac{\langle x, y \rangle}{\|x\| \|y\|}$$

B-1.3   Orthogonality

Two vectors are said to be orthogonal whenever their inner product is zero.

A system of vectors is said to be orthogonal whenever they are pairwise orthogonal. There can be at most n vectors in an orthogonal system, where n is the dimension of E.

A system of vectors is said to be orthonormal when it is orthogonal and the norm of each vector is 1.

Every Euclidean space has infinitely many orthonormal bases. In practice, given an arbitrary basis $(v_1, \dots, v_n)$, we can build an orthonormal basis $(v_1^*, \dots, v_n^*)$ by following Gram-Schmidt's orthonormalization process:

$$\begin{cases} v_1^* = v_1 / \|v_1\| \\ u_2 = v_2 - \langle v_1^*, v_2 \rangle v_1^*, \quad v_2^* = u_2 / \|u_2\| \\ \vdots \\ u_n = v_n - \sum_{i=1}^{n-1} \langle v_i^*, v_n \rangle v_i^*, \quad v_n^* = u_n / \|u_n\| \end{cases}$$

The orthogonal projection of a given vector x onto the line $\text{Span}(v)$ is simply $\frac{\langle x, v \rangle}{\|v\|^2} v$. In $\mathbb{R}^n$ with canonical inner product, the projection operator is then $P = \frac{vv^T}{v^T v}$.

Given an orthonormal basis $(v_1^*, \dots, v_n^*)$ the coordinates of a given vector x are $\langle x, v_i^* \rangle$ and we have $x = \sum_{i=1}^n \langle x, v_i^* \rangle v_i^*$.

An ortho*gonal* matrix O is a square matrix whose columns and rows are ortho*normal* vectors of $\mathbb{R}^n$; equivalently $OO^T = O^T O = I$, where I is the identity matrix.

Parseval's identity states that the norm of a vector does not depend on the orthonormal basis in which its coordinates are calculated:

$$\sum_{i=1}^n \langle x, v_i^* \rangle^2 = \|x\|^2$$

where $(v_1^*, \dots, v_n^*)$ is an arbitrary orthonormal basis of E.

B-2   SQUARE MATRIX DECOMPOSITIONS

Given a basis $B = (v_1, \dots, v_n)$ we may represent any linear transformation $f \colon E \to E$ as an $n \times n$ square matrix A whose columns are the coordinates of

$(f(v_1), \dots, f(v_n))$ in $\mathcal{B}$. Then $F \colon \mathbb{R}^n \to \mathbb{R}^n, x \mapsto Ax$ is an equivalent representation of f.

It is often useful to rewrite a given matrix as a product or sum of simpler components. For example, some matrices may be written $A = PDP^{-1}$ where P is an invertible square matrix whose columns are eigenvectors and D is a diagonal matrix of eigenvalues. By the spectral theorem, this is true of every symmetric matrix in which case P can be chosen to be orthogonal and we may write $A = \sum_{i=1}^{n} \lambda_i v_i^* v_i^{*T}$ where v^*'s are the columns of P. When all λ's are positive A is said to be positive-definite and when all λ's are nonnegative A is said to be positive-semidefinite.

Another type of decomposition is $A = LU$ where L is lower triangular and U is upper triangular. If A is symmetric positive-definite then we can find L, U such that $U = L^T$ and the decomposition $A = LL^T$ is called a Cholesky decomposition.

The bilinear transformation $B(x, y) = y^T A x$ defines an inner product on $\mathbb{R}^n$ if and only if A is symmetric positive-definite, in which case we may rewrite:

$$B(x, y) = \sum_{i=1}^{n} \lambda_i (y^T v_i^*)(v_i^{*T} x) = \|x\|_2 \|y\|_2 \sum_{i=1}^{n} \lambda_i \cos \widehat{(x, v_i^*)} \cos \widehat{(y, v_i^*)}$$

where $\|x\|_2 = \sqrt{x^T x}$ is the canonical norm and angles are measured canonically. The associated quantity $Q(x) = x^T A x = B(x, x) = \|x\|_2^2 \sum_{i=1}^{n} \lambda_i \cos^2 \widehat{(x, v_i^*)}$ is then known as a quadratic form.

The Rayleigh quotient $\mathfrak{R}(x) = \frac{x^T A x}{x^T x} = \frac{Q(x)}{\|x\|_2^2}$ measures the scaling factor between the canonical norm and the Q-norm; it can be shown to be comprised between $\min_i \lambda_i$ and $\max_i \lambda_i$. The maximum eigenvalue of A is then called the spectral radius $\rho(A)$, and we have $\|Ax\|_2^2 \le \rho(A^2) \|x\|_2^2$.

Solutions Manual

This Solutions Manual includes answers to all of the end of chapter problems found in this book (except for a few coding problems where the numerical answer is provided in the text).

CHAPTER 1: EXOTIC DERIVATIVES

1.1 "Free" Option

(a) The option is not really free because we may end up at a loss at and above the strike price. (See Figure S.1.)

(b) The replicating portfolio would include selling x digital calls struck at K at price p and buying a vanilla call struck at K for the premium of m. In order for the portfolio to have zero cost we must have $x \times p = m$.

(c) The cost of one digital call using the Black-Scholes model with the given parameters is $0.5398. The premium of the vanilla call from the Black-Scholes model is $7.97. Solving for x we get $\frac{7.97}{0.5398} = 14.76$.

1.2 Autocallable

Answer: $C \approx 12\%$.

1.3 Geometric Asian Option

(a) From Ito-Doeblin we have $\ln S_t = \ln S_0 + \alpha t + \sigma W_t$ where $\alpha = r - q - 1/2\sigma^2$. Substituting into the definition of A_T we get:

$$A_T = \exp\left(\frac{1}{T} \int_0^T \left[\ln S_0 + \alpha t + \sigma W_t \right] dt \right)$$

$$= \exp\left(\frac{1}{T} \left[T \ln S_0 + \frac{T^2}{2}\alpha + \sigma \int_0^T W_t dt \right] \right)$$

which yields the required expression for A_T after simplifications.

(b) From Ito-Doeblin, we get $d[(T - t)W_t] = -dW_t + (T - t)dW_t$, which yields the required result after integration of both sides over $[0, T]$.

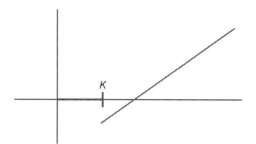

FIGURE S.1 "Free" option payoff.

The distribution of $\int_0^T (T-t)dW_t$ is thus normal with zero mean and variance $\int_0^T (T-t)^2 dt = \frac{1}{3}T^3$.

(c) Substituting $\hat{\sigma} = \sigma/\sqrt{3}$ and $\hat{q} = \frac{1}{2}\left(r+q+\frac{\sigma^2}{6}\right)$ we need to show that $\ln A_T$ is normally distributed with mean:

$$\ln S_0 + \left(r - \hat{q} - \frac{1}{2}\hat{\sigma}^2\right)T = \ln S_0 + \left[r - \frac{1}{2}\left(r+q+\frac{\sigma^2}{6}\right) - \frac{1}{2}\left(\frac{\sigma}{\sqrt{3}}\right)^2\right]T$$

$$= \ln S_0 + \frac{1}{2}\left(r - q - \frac{1}{2}\sigma^2\right)T$$

and variance $\frac{\sigma^2}{3}T$. Indeed the mean matches the expression from question (a), and using question (b) we find that the variance of $\frac{\sigma}{T}\int_0^T W_t dt$ is $\frac{\sigma^2}{T^2} \times \frac{1}{3}T^3 = \frac{\sigma^2}{3}T$ as required.

1.4 Change of Measure

We have $\mathbb{E}^Q(S_T) = \mathbb{E}^P\left(S_T \frac{dQ}{dP}\right)$ with $\frac{dQ}{dP} = \exp\left(\frac{r-\mu}{\sigma}W_T - \frac{1}{2}\left(\frac{r-\mu}{\sigma}\right)^2 T\right)$. Since $S_T = S_0 e^{\left(\mu - \frac{1}{2}\sigma^2\right)T + \sigma W_T}$ we have after substitution:

$$\mathbb{E}^Q(S_T) = \mathbb{E}^P\left\{S_0 \exp\left[\left(\mu - \frac{1}{2}\left(\sigma^2 + \left(\frac{r-\mu}{\sigma}\right)^2\right)\right)T + \left(\sigma + \frac{r-\mu}{\sigma}\right)W_T\right]\right\}$$

But $\mathbb{E}^P(\exp(\alpha W_T)) = e^{\alpha^2 T/2}$ and thus $\mathbb{E}^Q(S_T) = S_0 \exp\left[\left(\mu - \frac{1}{2}\left(\sigma^2 + \left(\frac{r-\mu}{\sigma}\right)^2\right)\right)T + \frac{1}{2}\left(\sigma + \frac{r-\mu}{\sigma}\right)^2 T\right]$. Expanding the second squared bracket and cancelling terms we are left with $\mathbb{E}^Q(S_T) = S_0 e^{rT}$ as required.

1.6 Siegel's Paradox

(a) Straightforward application of Ito-Doeblin.

(b) The "risk-neutral" dynamics of $1/X$ from question (a) correspond to the dollar risk-neutral measure, in which $1/X$ is non tradable (number of euros per dollar). The paradox is resolved by introducing the euro risk-neutral measure where $1/X$ follows the process:

$$d\frac{1}{X_t} = (r_{\mathbb{E}} - r_{\$})\frac{1}{X_t}dt + \sigma\frac{1}{X_t}d\tilde{W}_t$$

In the dollar risk-neutral measure, $1/X$ is the price of the dollar-euro exchange rate *quanto dollar*. Following the notations of Section 1-2.4 and defining $S = 1/X$, we have $\rho = -1$ and $\eta = \sigma$; thus the drift of S quanto dollar under the dollar risk-neutral measure is $r_{\mathbb{E}} - r_{\$} - \rho\sigma\eta = r_{\mathbb{E}} - r_{\$} + \sigma^2$ as required.

CHAPTER 2: THE IMPLIED VOLATILITY SURFACE

2.1 No Call or Put Spread Arbitrage Condition

We know the upper bound is:

$$\frac{\partial c}{\partial K} = \frac{\partial c_{BS}}{\partial K} + \frac{\partial c_{BS}}{\partial \sigma} \times \frac{\partial \sigma}{\partial K}$$

and we know that $\frac{\partial c}{\partial K} \leq 0$ so after rearranging terms we get:

$$\frac{\partial \sigma}{\partial K} \leq -\frac{\partial c_{BS}}{\partial K} \bigg/ \frac{\partial c_{BS}}{\partial \sigma}$$

We know the lower bound is:

$$\frac{\partial p}{\partial K} = \frac{\partial p_{BS}}{\partial K} + \frac{\partial p_{BS}}{\partial \sigma} \times \frac{\partial \sigma}{\partial K}$$

and we know that $\frac{\partial p}{\partial K} \geq 0$ so we get

$$\frac{\partial \sigma}{\partial K} \geq -\frac{\partial p_{BS}}{\partial K} \bigg/ \frac{\partial p_{BS}}{\partial \sigma}$$

From put-call parity: $c - p = S - Ke^{-rT}$, and thus:

- $\dfrac{\partial c_{BS}}{\partial K} = -e^{-rT}N(d_2)$ gives $\dfrac{\partial p_{BS}}{\partial K} = (1 - N(d_2))e^{-rT}$

- $\dfrac{\partial c_{BS}}{\partial \sigma} = \dfrac{\partial p_{BS}}{\partial \sigma} = e^{-rT}K\sqrt{T}N'(d_2)$

Putting them together we get:

$$U - L = -\frac{\frac{\partial c_{BS}}{\partial K}}{\frac{\partial c_{BS}}{\partial \sigma}} + \frac{\frac{\partial p_{BS}}{\partial K}}{\frac{\partial p_{BS}}{\partial \sigma}}$$

$$= \frac{e^{-rT} N(d_2)}{e^{-rT} K \sqrt{T} N'(d_2)} + \frac{e^{-rT}[1 - N(d_2)]}{e^{-rT} K \sqrt{T} N'(d_2)} = \frac{1}{K \sqrt{T} N'(d_2)}$$

Furthermore $KN'(d_2) = F_0 N'(d_2)$ and $N'(x) = \frac{1}{\sqrt{2\pi}} e^{-x^2/2}$

Thus:

$$U - L = \frac{1}{F_0 \sqrt{T} \frac{1}{\sqrt{2\pi}} e^{-\frac{d_1^2}{2}}} = \frac{\sqrt{2\pi} e^{d_1^2}}{F_0 \sqrt{T}}$$

as required.

2.2   No Butterfly Spread Arbitrage Condition

(a) Identities:

- We have:

$$\frac{\partial C}{\partial K} = -N(d_2(K)) = \int_{-\infty}^{d_2(K)} e^{-\frac{x^2}{2}} \frac{dx}{\sqrt{2\pi}}$$

Differentiating with respect to K:

$$\frac{\partial^2 C}{\partial K^2} = -d_2'(K) N'(d_2(K)) = -\frac{d}{dK} \left(\frac{\ln\left(\frac{S}{K}\right)}{\sigma \sqrt{T}} - \frac{\sigma^2 T}{2\sigma \sqrt{T}} \right) N'(d_2(K))$$

$$= -\frac{d}{dK} \left(\frac{\ln S}{\sigma \sqrt{T}} - \frac{\ln K}{\sigma \sqrt{T}} - \frac{\sigma^2 T}{2\sigma \sqrt{T}} \right) N'(d_2(K)) = \frac{N'(d_2)}{K \sigma \sqrt{T}}$$

as required.

- Differentiating $\frac{\partial C}{\partial K} = -N(d_2(K))$ with respect to σ:

$$\frac{\partial^2 C}{\partial \sigma \partial K} = \frac{\partial}{\partial K} (K \sqrt{T} N'(d_2))$$

Using the chain rule:

$$\frac{\partial}{\partial K}(K\sqrt{T}N'(d_2)) = \sqrt{T}N'(d_2) + K\sqrt{T}\frac{d}{dK}\{N'(d_2(K))\}$$

$$= \sqrt{T}N'(d_2) + K\sqrt{T}d_2'(K)N''(d_2(K))$$

But:

$$N''(d_2(K)) = \frac{-d_2}{\sqrt{2\pi}}e^{-d_2^2/2}$$

Substituting $d_2'(K)$ and $N''(d_2(K))$:

$$\sqrt{T}N'(d_2) + K\sqrt{T}d_2'(K)N''(d_2(K))$$

$$= \sqrt{T}N'(d_2) + K\sqrt{T}\frac{-1}{K\sigma\sqrt{T}}\frac{-d_2}{\sqrt{2\pi}}e^{-d_2^2/2}$$

Using the fact that $d_2 = d_1 - \sigma\sqrt{T}$, we get:

$$\frac{\partial^2 C}{\partial\sigma\partial K} = \frac{\sqrt{T}}{\sqrt{2\pi}}e^{\frac{-d_2^2}{2}} + \frac{d_2}{\sigma\sqrt{2\pi}}e^{\frac{-d_2^2}{2}}$$

$$= \left(\frac{\sigma\sqrt{T}}{\sigma\sqrt{2\pi}} + \frac{d_2}{\sigma\sqrt{2\pi}}\right)e^{\frac{-d_2^2}{2}} = \frac{d_1}{\sigma}N'(d_2)$$

- Differentiating $\frac{\partial C}{\partial\sigma} = K\sqrt{T}N'(d_2)$ with respect to σ:

$$\frac{\partial^2 C}{\partial\sigma^2} = K\sqrt{T}N''(d_2)d_2'(\sigma)$$

We have:

$$N''(d_2) = \frac{-d_2}{\sqrt{2\pi}}e^{-d_2^2/2}$$

and:

$$d_2'(\sigma) = \frac{d}{d\sigma}\left(\frac{\ln\left(\frac{S}{K}\right) - \sigma^2 T}{\sigma\sqrt{T}}\right) = \frac{-\ln\left(\frac{S}{K}\right)}{\sigma^2\sqrt{T}} - \frac{\sqrt{T}}{2}$$

Substituting back into $\frac{\partial^2 C}{\partial \sigma^2} = K\sqrt{T}N''(d_2)d_2'(\sigma)$:

$$\frac{\partial^2 C}{\partial \sigma^2} = K\sqrt{T}N'(d_2)\frac{-d_2}{\sqrt{2\pi}}e^{-d_2^2/2}\left(\frac{-\ln\left(\frac{S}{K}\right)}{\sigma^2\sqrt{T}} - \frac{\sqrt{T}}{2}\right)$$

$$= Kd_2\sqrt{T}N'(d_2)\left(\frac{\ln\left(\frac{S}{K}\right)}{\sigma^2\sqrt{T}} + \frac{\frac{1}{2}\sigma^2\sqrt{T}}{\sigma^2\sqrt{T}}\right)$$

Factoring by $\frac{1}{\sigma}$ and recognizing d_1 we obtain as required:

$$\frac{\partial^2 C}{\partial \sigma^2} = \frac{d_1 d_2}{\sigma}K\sqrt{T}N'(d_2)$$

(b) First-order derivative: $\varphi' = f_x + u'f_y$. Second-order derivative:

$$\varphi'' = (f_{xx} + u'f_{xy}) + \left[u''f_y + u' \times \left(f_{yx} + u'f_{yy}\right)\right]$$

which yields the required result after noting that $f_{xy} = f_{yx}$ by Schwarz's theorem.

(c) Applying the second-order chain rule:

$$\frac{\partial^2 c}{\partial K^2} = \frac{\partial^2 C}{\partial K^2} + 2\sigma^{*'}\frac{\partial^2 C}{\partial K \partial \sigma} + \sigma^{*'2}\frac{\partial^2 C}{\partial \sigma^2} + \sigma^{*''}\frac{\partial C}{\partial \sigma}$$

Substituting the identities from (a) we get the required result after further straightforward algebra.

(d) After simplifications $\frac{\partial^2 c}{\partial K^2} \geq 0$ is equivalent to:

$$2d_1\sigma^{*'}(K) + d_1 d_2\sigma^{*'2}(K) + \sigma^{*''}(K)\sigma^*(K) \geq -\frac{1}{K^2 T}$$

2.3 Sticky True Delta Rule

(a) Applying the chain rule: $\Delta(S) = \frac{\partial c_{BS}}{\partial S} + \sigma^{*'}(S)\frac{\partial c_{BS}}{\partial \sigma} = N(d_1) + \sigma^{*'}(S) \times K\sqrt{T}N'(d_2)$, whence the required result after substituting $K = 1$ and $T = 1$.

(b) If $\sigma^*(S) = a + b\Delta(S)$ then $\sigma^{*'}(S) = b\Delta'(S)$ and thus $\Delta = N(d_1) + b\Delta'N'(d_2)$ yielding the required result after appropriate substitutions.

(c) Because $\Delta' > 0$ (call delta goes up as S goes up) and $b < 0$ (volatility goes down as S and Δ go up) the sticky true delta rule would produce a lower delta than Black-Scholes.

CHAPTER 3: IMPLIED DISTRIBUTIONS

3.1   Overhedging Concave Payoffs

Assume $f(K_1) = 0$ for simplicity. From left to right: start with $f'(K_1)$ calls struck at K_1 so as to be tangential to the payoff; add $\alpha = \frac{f(K_3)-f'(K_1)(K_3-K_1)}{K_3-K_2}$ calls struck at K_2 such that the portfolio matches the payoff $f(K_3)$ at K_3; then add $\beta = f'(K_3) - f'(K_1) - \alpha$ calls struck at K_3 so as to be tangential to the payoff after K_3; and so on (see Figure S.2).

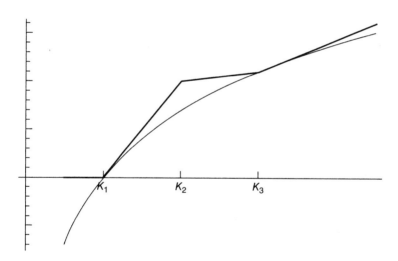

FIGURE S.2   Over-hedging concave payoffs.

3.2   Perfect Hedging with Puts and Calls

From Section 3-2:

$$f(S_T) = f(0) + f'(0)S_T + \int_0^\infty f''(K)\max(0, S_T - K)dK$$

Splitting the integral at F and using terminal put-call parity $c_T = S_T - K + p_T$ we get:

$$f(S_T) = f(0) + f'(0)S_T + \int_0^F f''(K)[(S_T - K) + p_T]dK + \int_F^\infty f''(K)c_T dK$$

$$= f(0) + f'(0)S_T + S_T \int_0^F f''(K)dK - \int_0^F f''(K)K dK$$

$$+ \int_0^F f''(K)p_T dK + \int_F^\infty f''(K)c_T dK$$

But $\int_0^F f''(K)dK = f'(F) - f'(0)$, and:

$$\int_0^F f''(K)K dK = [f'(K)K]_0^F - \int_0^F f'(K)dK = Ff'(F) - f(F) + f(0)$$

After substitutions and simplifications we get:

$$f(S_T) = [f(F) - f'(F)F] + f'(F)S_T + \int_0^F f''(K)\max(0, K - S_T)dK$$

$$+ \int_F^\infty f''(K)\max(0, S_T - K)dK$$

Thus:

$$f_0 = f(F)e^{-rT} + \int_0^F f''(K)p_0(K)dK + \int_F^\infty f''(K)c_0(K)dK$$

because $\mathbb{E}(S_T) = F$.

3.3 Implied Distribution and Exotic Pricing

(b)
- Answer: $\approx .1043$
- Answer: ≈ 1.0789
- Answer: $\approx .2693$
- Answer: $\approx .0211$. Vanilla overhedge with strikes 0.5, 0.9, 1, 1.1, 1.3, 1.7: Quantities are 0, 0, 0.0100, 0.1200, 0.6700, and 1.5200 (see Figure S.3).

(c) (i) Answer: approximately $0.8965.
(ii) Answer: approximately $0.8626.

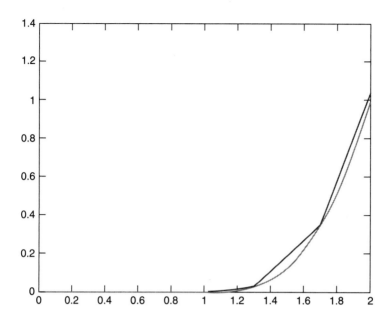

FIGURE 3.3

3.5 Path-Dependent Payoff

(a) For example: forward start option, Asian option.

(b) Pseudo-code:

    1. Loop for $i = 1$ to N:

        a. Generate and calculate $s_1 := S_0 \exp\left(\left(r - \frac{1}{2}\sigma^2\right) T_1 + \sigma\widetilde{\varepsilon}_1 \sqrt{T_1}\right)$

        b. Generate $\widetilde{\varepsilon}_1 \sim \mathcal{N}(0,1)$ and $\widetilde{\varepsilon}_2 \sim \mathcal{N}(0,1)$ independently and calculate

$$s_2 = s_1 \exp\left(\left(r - \frac{1}{2}\sigma^2\right)(T_2 - T_1) + \sigma\widetilde{\varepsilon}_2 \sqrt{T_2 - T_1}\right)$$

        c. Calculate $\text{Payoff}(i) = f(s_1, s_2)$

    2. Return $\frac{e^{-rT_2}}{N} \sum\limits_{i=1}^{N} Payoff(i)$

(c) We only know the marginal distributions of S_{T_1}, S_{T_2} but we are missing the conditional implied distribution of $S_{T_2} | S_{T_1}$.

3.6 Delta

From $\sigma^*(S_0, K) \equiv \sigma^*(K/S_0)$ we get $\frac{\partial \sigma^*}{\partial K} \equiv \frac{1}{S_0}\sigma^{*\prime}, \frac{\partial^2 \sigma^*}{\partial K^2} \equiv \frac{1}{S_0^2}\sigma^{*\prime\prime}$ and thus:

$$
\mathbb{P}\{S_T = K\} = \frac{N'(d_2)}{K\sigma^*\sqrt{T}} \left[1 + 2d_1 \left(\frac{K}{S_0}\sigma^{*\prime}\sqrt{T} \right) + d_1 d_2 \left(\frac{K}{S_0}\sigma^{*\prime}\sqrt{T} \right)^2 \right.
$$

$$
\left. + \left(\frac{K}{S_0}\sigma^{*\prime\prime}\sqrt{T} \right) \left(\frac{K}{S_0}\sigma^*\sqrt{T} \right) \right]
$$

```
atm_vol = SVI(1);
atm_vol1 = SVI(1/(1+epsilon));

price = 0;
for i=1:n
  normal = randn;
  x = exp(atm_vol*normal*sqrt(T) - 0.5*atm_vol^2*T);
  x1 = (1+epsilon)*exp(atm_vol1*normal*sqrt(T) - 0.5*atm_vol1^2*T);
  price = (i-1)/i*price + Payoff(x)*ImpDist(x) ...
          / lognpdf(x,-0.5*atm_vol^2*T,atm_vol*sqrt(T)) / i;
  price1 = (i-1)/i*price1 + Payoff(x1)*ImpDist(x1) ...
          / lognpdf(x1,-0.5*atm_vol1^2*T,atm_vol1*sqrt(T)) / i;
end
delta = price - price1
```

CHAPTER 4: LOCAL VOLATILITY AND BEYOND

4.1 From Implied to Local Volatility

(a) We rewrite Equation (4.1) by solving for $\frac{\partial C}{\partial T}$ after using the result from Problem 2.2(c) for $\frac{\partial^2 C}{\partial K^2}$.

$$
\sigma_{\text{loc}}^2(T, K) = \frac{\dfrac{\partial C}{\partial T}}{\dfrac{1}{2}K^2\dfrac{\partial^2 C}{\partial K^2}}
$$

$$
\frac{\partial^2 C}{\partial K^2} = \frac{N'(d_2)}{K\sigma^*(K)\sqrt{T}} \left[1 + 2d_1 \left(K\frac{\partial \sigma}{\partial K}\sqrt{T} \right) + d_1 d_2 \left(K\frac{\partial \sigma}{\partial K}\sqrt{T} \right)^2 \right.
$$

$$
\left. + \left(K\frac{\partial^2 \sigma}{\partial K^2}\sqrt{T} \right)(K\sigma^*(K)\sqrt{T}) \right]
$$

Take $C(K, T) = C_{BS}(S, K, T, \sigma^*(KT))$ and derive with respect to T:

$$\frac{\partial C}{\partial T} = \frac{\partial C_{BS}}{\partial T} + \frac{\partial \sigma^*}{\partial T}\frac{\partial C_{BS}}{\partial \sigma}$$

We are given $\frac{\partial C_{BS}}{\partial T}$ and $\frac{\partial C_{BS}}{\partial \sigma}$ so:

$$\frac{\partial C}{\partial T} = \frac{KN'(d_2)\sigma^*}{2\sqrt{T}} + \frac{\partial \sigma^*}{\partial T}K\sqrt{T}N'(d_2)$$

We then plug in $\frac{\partial C}{\partial T}$ and $\frac{\partial^2 C}{\partial K^2}$ into Equation (4.1):

$$\frac{\dfrac{KN'(d_2)\sigma^*}{2\sqrt{T}} + \dfrac{\partial \sigma^*}{\partial T}K\sqrt{T}N'(d_2)}{\dfrac{1}{2}K^2\dfrac{N'(d_2)}{K\sigma^*\sqrt{T}}} \times$$

$$\left[1 + 2d_1\left(K\frac{\partial \sigma^*}{\partial K}\sqrt{T}\right) + d_1 d_2\left(K\frac{\partial \sigma^*}{\partial K}\sqrt{T}\right)^2 + \left(K\frac{\partial^2 \sigma^*}{\partial K^2}\sqrt{T}\right)\left(K\sigma^*\sqrt{T}\right)\right]^{-1}$$

By dividing both numerator and denominator by $\frac{KN'(d_2)}{2\sigma^*\sqrt{T}}$, we obtain the desired Equation (4.2):

$$\sigma^2_{loc}(T, K) = \sigma^{*2}$$

$$\times \frac{1 + \dfrac{2T}{\sigma^*}\dfrac{\partial \sigma^*}{\partial T}}{1 + 2d_1\left(K\dfrac{\partial \sigma^*}{\partial K}\sqrt{T}\right) + d_1 d_2\left(K\dfrac{\partial \sigma^*}{\partial K}\sqrt{T}\right)^2 + \left(K\dfrac{\partial^2 \sigma^*}{\partial K^2}\sqrt{T}\right)(K\sigma^*\sqrt{T})}$$

(b) Replace $\sigma^2_{loc}(T, K)$ with $\sigma^2_{loc}(T)$ so we now have:

$$\sigma^{*2}(T)\frac{1 + \dfrac{2T}{\sigma^*}\dfrac{\partial \sigma^*}{\partial T}}{1 + 0 + 0 + 0} = \sigma^{*2}(T)\left(1 + \frac{2T}{\sigma^*}\frac{\partial \sigma^*}{\partial T}\right)$$

Now using the Hint:

$$\frac{d}{dT}(T\sigma^{*2}(T)) = 1 \times \sigma^{*2}(T) + T \times 2 \times \sigma^*(T)\frac{\partial \sigma^*}{\partial T} = \sigma^{*2}(T) + 2T\sigma^*(T)\frac{\partial \sigma^*}{\partial T}$$

$$= \sigma^{*2}(T)\left(1 + \frac{2T}{\sigma^*}\frac{\partial \sigma^*}{\partial T}\right)$$

Thus $\sigma_{\text{loc}}^2(T) = \sigma^{*2}(T)\left(1 + \frac{2T}{\sigma^*}\frac{\partial\sigma^*}{\partial T}\right)$ and by integration we find that:

$$\frac{1}{T}\int_0^T \sigma_{\text{loc}}^2(t, S_t)dt = \frac{1}{T}\int_0^T \frac{d}{dt}(t\sigma^{*2}(t))dt = \sigma^{*2}(T)$$

as required.

(c) To establish the hint, note that $\frac{\partial^2\sigma^*}{\partial K^2} = 0$ by linearity of σ^*, and substitute $d_2 = d_1 - \sigma^*\sqrt{T}$. Differentiating $\sigma_{\text{loc}}(K) \approx \frac{\sigma^*(K)}{1+d_1 K\sigma^{*\prime}(K)\sqrt{T}}$ with respect to K we obtain:

$$\sigma_{\text{loc}}{}'(K) \approx \frac{\sigma^{*\prime}(K)}{1 + d_1 K\sigma^{*\prime}(K)\sqrt{T}} + \sigma^*(K)\frac{-\frac{d}{dK}(d_1 K)}{(1 + d_1 K\sigma^{*\prime}(K)\sqrt{T})^2}\sigma^{*\prime}(K)\sqrt{T}$$

Near the money both denominators are close to 1; furthermore $d_1 = \frac{\ln(S/K)+\frac{1}{2}\sigma^{*2}T}{\sigma^*\sqrt{T}}$ gives $\frac{d}{dK}d_1 = -\frac{1}{K\sigma^*\sqrt{T}} - \frac{\ln(S/K)\sigma^{*\prime}\sqrt{T}}{\sigma^{*2}T} + \frac{1}{2}\sigma^{*\prime}\sqrt{T} \approx -\frac{1}{K\sigma^*\sqrt{T}} + \frac{1}{2}\sigma^{*\prime}\sqrt{T}$. After substitution and simplification:

$$\sigma_{\text{loc}}{}'(K) \approx \sigma^{*\prime}(K) + \sigma^{*\prime}(K)\left[1 - \frac{1}{2}\sigma^{*\prime}(K)T - d_1\sigma^{*\prime}(K)\sqrt{T}\right]$$

whose leading term is $2\sigma^{*\prime}(K)$.

4.2 Market Price of Volatility Risk

(a) The delta-hedged portfolio Π is long one option and short $\delta_S = \frac{\partial f}{\partial S}$ units of S. Thus:

$$d\Pi = df - \delta_S dS = \left(\gamma_{f,t}dt + \frac{\partial f}{\partial S}dS + \frac{\partial f}{\partial v}dv\right) - \delta_S dS$$

which yields the required result after cancelling terms.

(b) We have:

$$d\Pi_t - r\Pi_t dt = \left(\gamma_{f,t}dt + \frac{\partial f}{\partial v}dv\right) - r\left(f_t - \frac{\partial f}{\partial S}S_t\right)dt$$

$$= \left(\gamma_{f,t} - rf_t + r\frac{\partial f}{\partial S}S_t + \alpha_t\frac{\partial f}{\partial v}\right)dt + \omega_t\frac{\partial f}{\partial v}dZ_t$$

But $rf_t - rS_t\frac{\partial f}{\partial S} - \gamma_{f,t} = \Lambda_t\frac{\partial f}{\partial v}$ which yields the required result after substitution and simplifications.

(c) Conditional expectation: $\mathbb{E}_t\left(\frac{d\Pi_t}{\Pi_t}\right) = \left[r + \frac{\lambda_t \omega_t \frac{\partial f}{\partial v}}{\Pi_t}\right] dt$. Conditional standard deviation:

$$\sqrt{\mathbb{V}_t\left(\frac{d\Pi_t}{\Pi_t}\right)} = \frac{\omega_t \left|\frac{\partial f}{\partial v}\right|}{|\Pi_t|} dt$$

Thus $\mathbb{E}_t\left(\frac{d\Pi_t}{\Pi_t}\right) = rdt \pm \lambda_t \sqrt{\mathbb{V}_t\left(\frac{d\Pi_t}{\Pi_t}\right)}$, that is, at time t the risk-neutral expected return on the delta-hedged portfolio is the risk-free interest rate plus a positive or negative risk premium, which is proportional to the risk of the portfolio, with proportionality coefficient λ. This result applies to any option and λ is independent from the particular option chosen, which is why it is called the market price of volatility risk.

4.3 Local Volatility Pricing

(a) Figure S.4 shows a graph of the corresponding local volatility surface.
(b) Using Monte Carlo simulations:

- "Capped quadratic" option: $\min\left(1, \frac{S_1^2}{S_0^2}\right)$; answer: 0.76949

- Asian at-the-money-call: $\max\left(0, \frac{S_{0.25}+S_{0.5}+S_{0.75}+S_1}{4\times S_0} - 1\right)$; answer: 0.1242

- Barrier call: $\max(0, S_1 - S_0)$ if S always traded above 80 using 252 daily observations, 0 otherwise. Answer: 12.87577

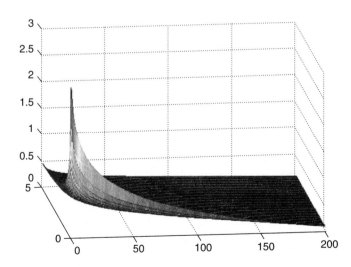

FIGURE S.4 Local volatility surface.

CHAPTER 5: VOLATILITY DERIVATIVES

5.1 Delta-Hedging P&L Simulation

(a) Positive Path: See Figure S.5
Negative Path: See Figure S.5
(b) Average P&L: −$11,663.80 (see Figure S.6)

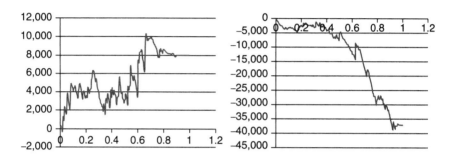

FIGURE S.5 Cumulative P&L: positive and negative paths.

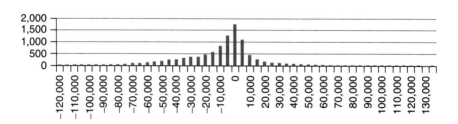

FIGURE S.6 Distribution of final cumulative P&L.

5.2 Volatility Trading with Options

(a) (i) If σ is constant then Cumulative P&L $= \frac{1}{2}(\sigma^2 - \sigma^{*2})\int_0^T e^{r(T-t)}\Gamma_t S_t^2 dt$.
For a vanilla call $\Gamma > 0$ and thus the cumulative P&L is always positive.

(ii) We have Cumulative P&L $= \frac{1}{2}\int_0^T e^{r(T-t)}\mathbb{E}[\Gamma_t S_t^2(\sigma_t^2 - \sigma^{*2})]dt$. By iterated expectations:

$$\mathbb{E}\left[\Gamma_t S_t^2\left(\sigma_t^2 - \sigma^{*2}\right)\right] = \mathbb{E}\left[\Gamma_t S_t^2 \mathbb{E}_t\left(\sigma_t^2 - \sigma^{*2}\right)\right] > 0$$

(b) The aggregate cumulative P&L is:

$$\frac{q_1}{2}\int_0^T e^{r(T-t)}\Gamma_t^{(1)}S_t^{(1)2}\left[\sigma_t^{(1)2} - \sigma^{*(1)2}\right]dt + \frac{q_2}{2}\int_0^T e^{r(T-t)}\Gamma_t^{(2)}S_t^{(2)2}\left[\sigma_t^{(2)2} - \sigma^{*(2)2}\right]dt$$

As a sum of two independent normal distributions the aggregate distribution is normal with parameters:

- Mean: $q_1 m_1 + q_2 m_2$
- Standard deviation: $\sqrt{q_1^2 s_1^2 + q_2^2 s_2^2} \le (q_1 + q_2)\max(s_1, s_2)$

This result sheds light on the diversification effect obtained by delta-hedging several options within an option book: the expected income is the sum of individual delta-hedging P&Ls, but it is less risky than delta-hedging a single position.

5.4 Generalized Variance Swaps

(a) From Ito-Doeblin: $d[g(S_t)] = g'(S_t)dS_t + \frac{1}{2}g''(S_t)\sigma_t^2 S_t^2 dt$. But $g''(S) = \frac{f(S)}{S^2}$; rearranging terms we get: $\frac{1}{2}f(S_t)\sigma_t^2 dt = d[g(S_t)] - g'(S_t)dS_t$. Integrating over $[0, T]$ yields the desired result.

Thus generalized variance may be replicated by a combination of cash, two derivative contracts paying off $g(S_T)$ at maturity, and dynamically trading S to maintain a short position of $2g'(S_t)$ at all times. Taking expectations we find that the fair value is:

$$\mathbb{E}\left(\int_0^T f(S_t)\sigma_t^2 dt\right) = 2\mathbb{E}[g(S_T)] - 2g(S_0) = 2(g_0 - g(S_0))$$

since $\mathbb{E}(dW_t) = 0$.

(b) From Problem 3.2 we get: $g_0 = g(S_0) + \int_0^{S_0} g''(K)p_0(K)dK + \int_{S_0}^\infty g''(K) \times c_0(K)dK$ whence the required formula after substituting $g''(K) = \frac{f(K)}{K^2}$ and annualizing.

(c) For the corridor varswap $K_{gvar} = \sqrt{\frac{2}{T}\left(\int_L^{S_0}\frac{1}{K^2}p(K)dK + \int_{S_0}^U\frac{1}{K^2}c(K)dK\right)}$

5.5   Call on Realized Variance

(a) Solving for v_t we have: $v_t = v_0 \exp\left(-2\omega^2 \int_0^T \left(\frac{T-t}{T}\right)^2 dt + 2\omega \int_0^T \frac{T-t}{T} dW_t\right)$

Thus v_t is lognormally distributed with mean $-2\omega^2 \int_0^T \left(\frac{T-t}{T}\right)^2 dt = -\frac{2}{3}\omega^2 T$ and standard deviation $\frac{2}{\sqrt{3}}\omega\sqrt{T}$. From Black's formula we have $\text{Varcall}_0 = e^{-rT}[v_0 N(d_1) - KN(d_2)]$ where $d_{1,2} = \frac{\ln(v_0/K) \pm \frac{2}{3}\omega^2 T}{2\omega\sqrt{T/3}}$. At the money this simplifies to $\text{Varcall}_0 = v_0 e^{-rT}[N(\omega\sqrt{T/3}) - N(-\omega\sqrt{T/3})]$ which yields the required formula because $N(x) - N(-x) = 2N(x) - 1$.

(b) For $x \approx 0$ we have $N(x) \approx N(0) + xN'(0)$.

CHAPTER 6: INTRODUCING CORRELATION

6.1   Lower Bound for Average Correlation

(a) Substitute $x = e$ in $\hat{\rho}_R(x) \le \frac{1}{n}\lambda_n/\cos^2\widehat{(x,e)}$.

(b) Because $\hat{\rho}_R(\alpha x) = \hat{\rho}_R(x)$ we have $\min_{x \in \mathbb{R}^n} \hat{\rho}_R(x) = \min_{x \in \mathbb{R}^n; x^T e = 1} (x^T R x)$. Define the Lagrangian $\mathcal{L}(x, \lambda) = x^T R x - \lambda(e^T x - 1)$. The first-order condition yields $2x^T R = -\lambda e^T$ that is, $x = \frac{1}{2}\lambda R^{-1} e$. The constraint $e^T x = 1$ then gives the value of λ and we get the required result after substitution and simplification.

(c) (i) By spectral decomposition: $e^T R e = \sum_{i=1}^n \lambda_i (v_i^T e)^2$, $e^T R^{-1} e = \sum_{i=1}^n \lambda_i^{-1}(v_i^T e)^2$. Furthermore, Parseval's identity states that $\sum_{i=1}^n (v_i^T x)^2 = x^T x$ for any x, and thus $\sum_{i=1}^n (v_i^T e)^2 = n$. Scaling by appropriate constants we obtain the required result.

(ii) Rewrite $A = \sum_{i=1}^{n-1} \alpha_i \lambda_i + \alpha_n \lambda_n$ and make the approximation that for $i = 1, \ldots, n - 1$:

$$\alpha_i \approx \frac{1}{n-1}\sum_{j=1}^{n-1} \alpha_j = \frac{1}{n-1}(1 - \alpha_n)$$

which is justified by the fact that $\alpha_n \approx 1$ since v_n and e are assumed to form a tight angle. Proceed similarly for H.

6.2 Geometric Basket Call

(a) We have:

$$\ln b_T = \sum_{i=1}^{n} w_i \ln \frac{S_T^{(i)}}{S_0^{(i)}} = \sum_{i=1}^{n} w_i \left[\left(\mu_i - \frac{1}{2}\sigma_i^2 \right) T + \sigma_i W_T^{(i)} \right]$$

$$= \sum_{i=1}^{n} w_i \left(\mu_i - \frac{1}{2}\sigma_i^2 \right) T + \sum_{i=1}^{n} w_i \sigma_i W_T^{(i)}$$

where $\mu_i = \frac{1}{T} \ln \frac{F^{(i)}}{S_0^{(i)}}$ is the annualized risk-neutral drift of $S^{(i)}$. As a sum of normal variables $\ln b_T$ is normally distributed with mean $m = \sum_{i=1}^{n} w_i \left(\mu_i - \frac{1}{2}\sigma_i^2 \right) T$ and variance:

$$v = \mathbb{V}\left(\sum_{i=1}^{n} w_i \sigma_i W_T^{(i)} \right) = \sum_{i=1}^{T} w_i^2 \sigma_i^2 T + 2 \sum_{i<j} w_i w_j \sigma_i \sigma_j \rho_{i,j} T$$

(b) $price = e^{-rT} \mathbb{E}\left[\max\left(0, e^{m + \tilde{\epsilon}\sqrt{v}} - k \right) \right] = e^{-rT + \frac{1}{2}v} \mathbb{E}\left[\max\left(0, e^{m - \frac{1}{2}v + \tilde{\epsilon}\sqrt{v}} - k' \right) \right]$

where $k' = ke^{-\frac{1}{2}v}$. Using Black's formula: $price = e^{-rT + v/2}[e^m N(d_1) - k' N(d_2)]$ with $d_{1,2} = \frac{m - \ln k' \pm \frac{1}{2}v}{\sqrt{v}}$. Further simplifications are possible.

6.4 Continuously Monitored Correlation

After substitution, we have by Cauchy-Schwarz:

$$c = \frac{\int_0^T \sigma_t^{(1)} \sigma_t^{(2)} \rho_{1,2} dt}{\sqrt{\int_0^T [\sigma_t^{(1)}]^2 dt \times \int_0^T [\sigma_t^{(2)}]^2 dt}} = \rho_{1,2} \frac{\langle \sigma^{(1)}, \sigma^{(2)} \rangle}{\|\sigma^{(1)}\| \cdot \|\sigma^{(2)}\|} \le \rho_{1,2},$$

where $\langle f, g \rangle = \int_0^T f(t)g(t)dt$.

CHAPTER 7: CORRELATION TRADING

7.1

(a) $\beta_0 = \dfrac{\text{Straddle}_0^{\text{Basket}}}{\sum_{i=1}^{n} w_i \times \text{Straddle}_0^{(i)}}$ is positive because straddles always have a positive payoff and thus price. It must be less than 1 because of the triangle inequality: $\left| \sum_{i=1}^{n} w_i S_T^{(i)} / S_0^{(i)} - k \right| \leq \sum_{i=1}^{n} w_i \left| S_T^{(i)} / S_0^{(i)} - k \right|$

(b) Use the proxy $\text{Straddle}_0^{ATMF} \approx \dfrac{2}{\sqrt{2\pi}} S_0 \sigma^* \sqrt{T}$

7.2

(a) From the Black-Scholes PDE $\frac{1}{2}\sigma^2 \Gamma_t S_t^2 = -\Theta_t$. Applying Ito-Doeblin to Θ:
$d\left[\frac{1}{2}\sigma^2 \Gamma_t S_t^2 \right] = -d\Theta_t = -\left[\frac{\partial \Theta_t}{\partial t} dt + \frac{\partial \Theta_t}{\partial S} dS_t + \frac{1}{2} \frac{\partial^2 \Theta_t}{\partial S^2} (dS_t)^2 \right]$. Taking expectations we get:

$$\mathbb{E}_t d\left[\frac{1}{2}\sigma^2 \Gamma_t S_t^2 \right] = -\left[\frac{\partial \Theta_t}{\partial t} + \frac{1}{2} \frac{\partial^2 \Theta_t}{\partial S^2} \sigma^2 S_t^2 \right] dt$$

which vanishes because Greeks must also satisfy the Black-Scholes PDE.

7.3

At time 0 the portfolio value is $\sigma_{\text{Basket}}^{\star 2} - \beta \sum_{i=1}^{n} w_i \sigma_i^{\star 2}$, and the vega of each component is $\frac{\partial(\sigma^{\star 2})}{\partial \sigma^\star} = 2\sigma^\star$. Hence the portfolio vega is $2\sigma_{\text{Basket}}^\star - 2\beta \sum_{i=1}^{n} w_i \sigma_i^\star = 2\sigma_{\text{Basket}}^\star - 2 \dfrac{\sigma_{\text{Basket}}^\star}{\sum_{i=1}^{n} w_i \sigma_i^\star} \sum_{i=1}^{n} w_i \sigma_i^\star = 0$.

CHAPTER 8: LOCAL CORRELATION

8.1 Implied Correlation

Implied correlation is constant iff $\frac{d}{dk}\left[\frac{a(k)}{b(k)} \right]^2 = 0$, i.e., iff $2\left[\frac{a(k)}{b(k)} \right] \frac{a'(k)b(k) - a(k)b'(k)}{b^2(k)} = 0$, whence the required result after simplifications.

8.2 Dynamic Local Correlation I

When $D = I$ and $U = ee^T$ Langnau's alpha is:

$$\alpha = \frac{\left(\sigma_{\text{Basket}}^{\text{loc}}\right)^2 B_t^2 - y^T I y}{y^T (ee^T) y - y^T I y} = \frac{\left(\sigma_{\text{Basket}}^{\text{loc}}\right)^2 B_t^2 - y^T y}{(y^T e)^2 - y^T y}$$

where $y_i = w_i \sigma_i^{\text{loc}}(t, S_t^{(i)}) S_t^{(i)}$. Define $x_i = \frac{w_i S_t^{(i)}}{B_t}$ and divide both the numerator and denominator of the above expression by B to get:

$$\alpha = \frac{\left(\sigma_{\text{Basket}}^{\text{loc}}\right)^2 - \sum_{i=1}^n x_i^2 \sigma_i^{\text{loc}\,2}}{\left(\sum_{i=1}^n x_i \sigma_i^{\text{loc}}\right)^2 - \sum_{i=1}^n x_i^2 \sigma_i^{\text{loc}\,2}} = \rho(x)$$

It is easy to verify that $\sum_{i=1}^n x_i = 1$.

CHAPTER 9: STOCHASTIC CORRELATION

9.2

(a) The process clearly remains within $[0,1]$ because it is continuous and its drift and volatility coefficients vanish at 0 and 1. Let us show that the bound 0 is nonattracting:

$$s(y) = \exp\left(-\int_{y_0}^y \frac{2\omega^2 x (1-x)}{x^2 \omega^2 (1-x)^2/(1-x/2)} dx\right) = \exp\left(-\int_{y_0}^y \frac{2-x}{x(1-x)} dx\right)$$

$$= \exp\left(-[2\ln x - \ln(1-x)]_{y_0}^y\right) = \left(\frac{y}{y_0}\right)^{-2}\left(\frac{1-y}{1-y_0}\right)$$

Thus $\lim_{x\downarrow 0} \int_{x_0}^x s(y)dy = \infty$ since $\int_0^{x_0} \frac{dy}{y^2}$ diverges. A similar analysis shows that the bound 1 is also nonattracting.

(b) We want to find $f(x)$, $g(x)$ such that:

$$dx/x = (g^2 - fgh)dt + \sqrt{f^2 - 2fgh + g^2}\, dB_t.$$

Thus we must solve:

$$\begin{cases} g^2 - fgh = \omega^2 (1 - x) \\ f^2 - 2fgh + g^2 = \omega^2 \dfrac{(1 - x)^2}{1 - x/2} \end{cases}$$

Taking ratios we get $\frac{g^2 - fgh}{f^2 - 2fgh + g^2} = \frac{1 - x/2}{1 - x}$; dividing both numerator and denominator by g^2 on the left-hand side we obtain $\frac{1 - ph}{p^2 - 2ph + 1} = \frac{1 - x/2}{1 - x}$. Solving for p after substituting $h = \sqrt{x(2 - x)}$ we find $p = \sqrt{\frac{x}{2-x}}$, that is, $f = g\sqrt{\frac{x}{2-x}}$. Substituting in $g^2 - fgh = \omega^2(1 - x)$ and simplifying we get $g^2 = \omega^2$, and thus $f = \omega\sqrt{\frac{x}{2-x}}$.

(c) This model is not suitable for several reasons: it has only one parameter ω, which leaves little freedom for parameterization, and the volatility of basket variance f is *lower* than the volatility of constituent variance g, which is contrary to empirical observation.

Author's Note

This is a book about finance, intended for professionals and future professionals. I am not trying to sell you any security, or give you any investment advice. The views expressed here are solely mine and do not necessarily reflect those of any entity directly or indirectly related to me. I took great care in proofreading this book, but I disclaim any responsibility for any remaining errors and any use to which the contents of this book is put. Some chapters contain original research material whose accuracy cannot be guaranteed.

About the Author

Sébastien Bossu is currently Principal at Ogee Group LLC where he runs the Ogee Structured Opportunities fund, which posted a 29.8 percent net return in 2012–2013. He has almost 10 years' experience in banking and the financial industry at institutions such as J.P. Morgan, Dresdner Kleinwort, and Goldman Sachs. An expert in derivative securities, Sébastien has published several papers and textbooks in the field and is a regular speaker at international conferences.

Sébastien is currently an Adjunct Professor at Pace University and was recently inducted into the 2014 edition of *Who's Who in America*, published by Marquis. He is a graduate from the University of Chicago, HEC Paris, Columbia University, and Université Pierre et Marie Curie, and he previously taught at Fordham University, HEC Paris, and Université Paris-7.

Index